D0584118

William Harvey

And the Mechanics of the Heart

Owen Gingerich
General Editor

William Harvey

And the Mechanics of the Heart

Jole Shackelford

OXFORD
UNIVERSITY PRESS

OXFORD
UNIVERSITY PRESS

Oxford   New York
Auckland Bangkok Buenos Aires Cape Town Chennai
Dar es Salaam Delhi Hong Kong Istanbul Karachi Kolkata
Kuala Lumpur Madrid Melbourne Mexico City Mumbai
Nairobi São Paulo Shanghai Taipei Tokyo Toronto

Copyright © 2003 by Jole Shackelford

Published by Oxford University Press, Inc.
198 Madison Avenue, New York, New York 10016
www.oup-usa.org

Oxford is a registered trademark of Oxford University Press

All rights reserved. No part of this publication may be reproduced,
stored in a retrieval system, or transmitted, in any form or by any means,
electronic, mechanical, photocopying, recording, or otherwise,
without the prior permission of Oxford University Press.

Library of Congress Cataloging-in-Publication Data
Shackelford, Jole.
  William Harvey and the mechanics of the heart / Jole Shackelford.
      p. cm. — (Oxford portraits in science)
Summary: A biography of the eminent seventeenth century physician and
scientist who discovered the functions of the heart, arteries, and veins
in the circulation of blood.
Includes bibliographical references and index.
  ISBN 0-19-512049-3 (alk. paper)
  1. Harvey, William, 1578-1657—Juvenile literature. 2.
Physiologists—England—Biography—Juvenile literature. 3.
Physicians—England—Biography—Juvenile literature. 4.
Blood—Circulation—History—Juvenile literature. [1. Harvey, William,
1578-1657. 2. Physicians. 3. Blood—Circulation—History.] I. Title.
II. Series.
  QP26.H3 S53 2003
  612.1'092—dc21
                                        2003007746

Printing number: 9 8 7 6 5 4 3 2 1

Printed in the United States of America
on acid-free paper

On the cover: Eighteenth-century portrait of William Harvey by James MacArdell. Inset:
William Harvey by an unknown artist, probably painted toward the end of Harvey's life.
Frontispiece: This copper plate engraving of William Harvey by artist Wilhelm von Bemmel
was engraved by Jacobus Houbraken and published in 1739.

Contents

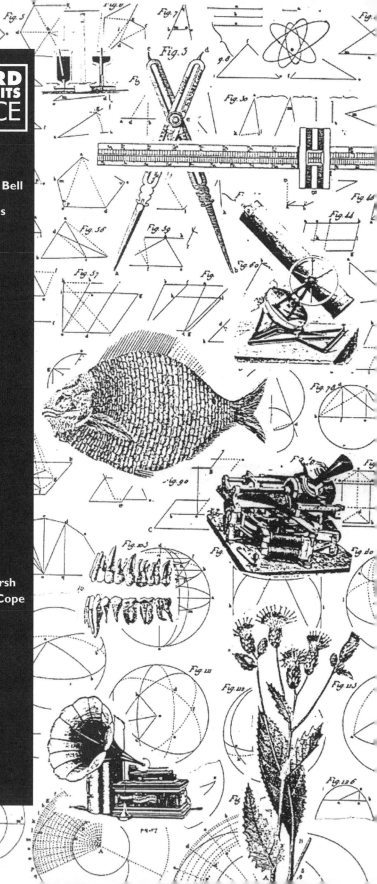

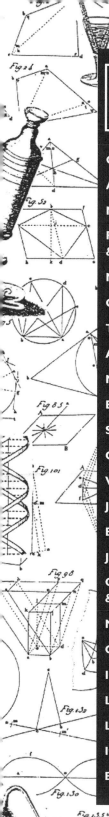

OXFORD PORTRAITS IN SCIENCE

Introduction

You are a student at one of the world's best universities, beginning to master texts that will enable you to become a licensed medical doctor, an M.D. It is 1600, and the university you are attending is in northern Italy. You have perhaps heard that Giordano Bruno, a renegade monk who was spreading unacceptable ideas about Christ, God, and nature, was tied to a stake in the flower-market square in Rome and publicly burned to death last February. You do not approve, but you understand that this is a reactionary measure, undertaken by Catholic authorities who are alarmed by the spread of new religious ideas and fear a breakdown of order in Europe.

It has been more than three quarters of a century since Martin Luther nailed up a list of grievances against the church and started a Protestant rebellion. Now there are Lutherans, Calvinists, Anabaptists, Mennonites, and all manner of religious groups that defy the Pope and the Catholic church. And they are all fighting among themselves, each convinced that they hold the truth. Trouble is brewing in central Europe, where shifting allegiances are creating an unstable political situation. And it has not been much more than a couple of decades since the St. Bartholomew's Day Massacre in France, a frenzy during which the predominant French Catholics attempted to rid the country of many of its Protestants. Still, many remain, especially in the south. Soon their political leader will become the next King of France. What will happen then?

In England, your homeland, the Protestant Queen Elizabeth is getting old, unmarried and without children. Who will succeed her? Will a Catholic member of her family occupy the throne of England and attempt to revive the religious per-secutions carried out by her sister Queen Mary? King James VI of Scotland has the best claim on the English crown, and although he is a Calvinist, his mother was a staunch Catholic who was executed by her cousin Queen Elizabeth. What will he do if he becomes the next king of England? To confuse matters further, he recently married the daughter of the king of Denmark, who is a convinced Lutheran.

Surely troubled times lie ahead. However, you must think about the task before you which is to study hard so that you can pass your exams and avoid public humiliation during the many disputations in which you will be asked to participate. A formal disputation will require you to represent and defend a considered point of view in an oral discussion of a selected topic, usually one that is disputed in the various textbooks. Disputations are grueling exercis-es designed to sharpen one's wits and debating skills. Tonight you must again focus your thoughts on the funda-mentals of human physiology, the understanding of how the body and its parts function, upon which all medical theory and practice depends.

You learn that the food we eat is broken down in our stomach by a process likened to cooking. The digested material then passes into the intestines, where it is separated from the waste matter and is diverted to the liver, which further refines it into blood. From the liver, nutrient-rich blood is drawn out through veins into the various parts of the body, which attract it to supply their growth and main-tenance. Some of the blood reaches the right side of the heart via a large vein, and filters through a thick wall of tis-sue to the left side. There it is mixed with some sort of air or energizing substance that comes into the heart from the lungs and is distributed to the body through the arteries, providing warmth, energy, and vitality to our parts. It all makes good sense.

After all, the ancient Greeks had perceived that there was a physical difference between the veins and the arteries 2,000 years ago. The arteries are tougher than the veins, and are made of different layers of tissue. Furthermore, the arteries pulsate, and the nature of a person's pulse correlates with his state of health. Entire volumes have been written on how to diagnose a patient's illness by examining the pulse. If veins and arteries have such different structures, what is more natural than to assume that they perform different functions? The veins distribute nutrient, which ebbs and flows sluggishly through the body, and the arteries are alive, pulsating with vitality and warming the body. It all makes sense . . . in 1600.

Today we understand things differently. We now know that blood circulates in our bodies, and continually provides nutrients and oxygen for the reactions that give us warmth and energy to move, while also carrying away the waste products of the chemical processes that take place in our countless cells. Blood has an important place in our concept of health, disease, and healing. Physicians advise us to exercise vigorously to improve our heart and circulation. When we become ill, we are likely to have a sample of blood tested to determine the nature of our sickness. If drugs are administered to help us heal, it is quite possible that they will be injected; if we are seriously ill, they will be delivered intravenously (directly to the veins). If our kidneys fail, our blood will be cleansed of impurities by a machine. Both our understanding of how the body works and the means we use to heal it depend on our knowledge that the blood is pumped through the body by the heart: blood flows from the heart into the arteries and into the capillaries in the body's tissues; then into the veins and back to the heart. In this process, the blood is circulated through the lungs, where it loses the carbon dioxide that has built up and receives fresh oxygen, which gives it again a bright red color. None of this would have made much sense to the medical student of 1600. What changed? When did it change? How long did it take for people to accept that the old theories of the body were wrong?

Much of the credit for introducing the idea that the blood circulates though the body is given to William Harvey. He was a student of medicine in 1600 and mastered the traditional theory of human physiology as well as all the scientific theory and medical practice that depended on it and supported it. Yet sometime between 1616 and 1628, he became convinced that the old theory was wrong, and he set about demonstrating to himself and to the world that the heart's main purpose was to circulate the blood. He has been called a revolutionary for helping to introduce a new way of thinking about scientific evidence and constructing scientific practice. However, he caused a revolution not by scrapping tradition, but by pursuing a research program that was in some respects shaped by the ancient Greeks. He organized his arguments in the way that he and every other philosopher and physician had been taught in school. Yet something about his procedure was different.

Acceptance of new scientific ideas depends not only on scientists' ability to understand them, but also on their social, religious, and political beliefs. This was true in Harvey's day and it is true in our own. However, his choice of certain methods of research and presentation of results succeeded in making "natural philosophy"—what we now term science—persuasive in a way that helped free scientific argument from broader philosophical and religious concerns.

This revolution was part of a broader transformation of scientific thinking and practice that completely rearranged the intellectual world of Europe. The dramatic change, which historians have called the Scientific Revolution, did not occur in a vacuum, but was shaped by the historical context in which Harvey and his contemporaries worked. The history of William Harvey's medical speculations and his experimental approach to scientific argumentation reveals the beginnings of this revolution in medicine and biology. Much of our current scientific practice depends on the methods and practices laid down in William Harvey's lifetime, and by examining these practices we can learn something about the roots of our science.

A Young Physician in Shakespeare's England

William Harvey was born in Folkestone, a small fishing village on the English Channel, not far from Dover. It was an old town, dating back to Roman times, and because of its location it was well positioned for commerce—both legal shipping and smuggling. His father, Thomas Harvey, became a successful businessman by taking advantage of the increased trade with the European continent in the late 16th century. In 1586 Thomas Harvey was elected alderman of Folkestone, and in 1600, mayor. He married Joan Hawke in 1577, and together they had nine children, the oldest of whom was William, who was born on the first day of April in 1578.

William began his formal education at Mr. Johnson's school in Folkestone, and in 1588 he was admitted to the King's grammar school in Canterbury where he learned to read and write Latin proficiently and also to declaim in good classical Latin. Latin was the common language of all European courts and universities, and its mastery was essential

This 1860 image of East Weir Bay near Folkestone in Kent, England, gives an idea of what the coastline near Harvey's home looked like in his lifetime.

for advanced study of any kind. During declamation students argued a proposition publicly according to established principles. It was an ever-present part of academic life and Harvey's polished skill in declamation shaped his lectures and published writings throughout his life.

Canterbury holds a prominent place in English history. Legend has it that the cathedral at Canterbury was founded by Augustine, apostle to the English, soon after he brought Christianity to the island in 598. Schools were administratively attached to Europe's cathedrals in the Middle Ages. Canterbury, as the seat of the English church, was the first cathedral in England to get such a school. So when Thomas Harvey sent his son to study at King's School in Canterbury, he was placing him in one of the best funded and most venerable schools in the realm.

Although attendance at a grammar school was becoming more common during the late 16th century, especially among members of England's growing middle class, which included the Harveys, education of any sort was a privilege. By 1600 about one out of three adult males was literate in English, and the ability to read and write Latin was even less common. Aristocratic boys, and sometimes girls, were usually taught at home by a private tutor. For boys of Harvey's social class, sons of merchants and tradesmen, schooling was usually done at local schools and grammar schools followed by an apprenticeship. Education for middle-class girls was rarer and usually done in the home using self-instruction manuals.

King's School in Canterbury reserved places for exceptionally able but poor students, who were supported at the Church's expense. It also took in students of financial means. William was not listed among those students dependent on the church, so he was probably supported by his father and lived with his uncle, who resided in Canterbury. It is likely that Thomas Harvey placed his first-born son into such an elite school to determine if he were suited to university education and a higher professional calling, rather than joining the family business in merchandising and international trade, which in time occupied five of his six brothers. The remaining brother entered service to the court of King James as a footman.

William finished school at 15 and proceeded to attend university. In principle, admission to higher education in medieval Europe depended chiefly upon scholastic ability. A family's wealth was often less crucial to obtaining entrance to the university than was the family's connection with the Church. Students were financially supported by Church patronage or, if an advanced student, by teaching undergraduates, tutoring, or other activities.

In England, Henry VIII's reformation of the church during 1536–39 deprived it of many sources of income that had been used to support scholars, and a university education increasingly depended upon family wealth, the patronage of an aristocrat, or an award of a scholarship. In Harvey's day and for long afterward, attendance at an English university was exceptional, amounting to somewhere around three or four thousand undergraduates at any one time in the whole country, and they were usually members of the gentry, or middle class. Of them, about a third left without taking a degree.

In the 16th century, there were two universities in England, both of which were already very old. The university at Oxford was one of the first in Europe, dating back to the late 12th century, when universities were first being founded. Cambridge University, where Harvey intended to study, was only slightly newer, having been established in the early 13th century. Neither university was particularly well known for its medical curriculum, but one of the colleges at Cambridge, called Gonville and Caius College, attracted students who desired to study medicine. Compared with the great European universities that taught medicine—Paris and Montpellier in France and Bologna and Padua in Italy—Cambridge's medical curriculum was unsophisticated, but it was perhaps the best England had to offer.

One particularly attractive feature offered at Cambridge University was the Matthew Parker Scholarship in medicine, which was specifically intended to support a student from the shire of Kent who had studied at King's School at Canterbury. William Harvey fit the requirements exactly and was awarded the scholarship. It provided tuition, board, and spending money for six years' residence at Gonville and Caius College. Without this support, he would likely have had to go into the family business and help his father support their growing family. He enrolled on May 31, 1593. Except for a few extended absences (possibly because of illness) toward the end of his residence, he spent most of the next six years studying at Cambridge.

Up to that point William Harvey's career path followed that of another well-known Englishman from the period, Christopher Marlowe. Marlowe, said to be the first great English poet-playwright, had graduated from King's School

This 1690 engraving shows Caius and Gonville College behind the Gate of Honour in the foreground. The campus must have looked much like this when Harvey studied medicine there in the late 1590s.

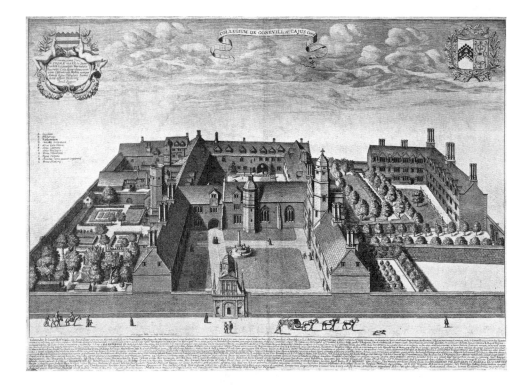

in Canterbury in 1580 and had also held a Parker scholarship at Cambridge. He went to London, where he wrote the plays that transformed English drama and paved the way for his much more famous friend and contemporary, William Shakespeare. Unfortunately, Marlowe's creative career was cut short by his murder in a pub the day before Harvey enrolled at Cambridge.

The biography and plays of Shakespeare, perhaps more than those by any other well-known English figure from the time, reflect the world in which William Harvey spent most of his adult life. Life in turn-of-the-century London—on the streets, at the English Court, and in the great aristocratic houses—is amply mirrored in Shakespeare's work.

England's population had increased dramatically through the 16th and 17th centuries, causing a relative oversupply of labor, a rise in agricultural prices, and a rise in land rents. The result was that the poor became poorer, and by the early 1600s, they were living with the constant threat of food shortages. Meanwhile, the land-owning aristocracy and the growing middle class that provided to the people goods from overseas and professional services prospered.

With prosperity came new construction, transforming the seats of England's great estates into elaborate and ornate, neoclassical country houses. The rich also began to build houses in London, where they might spend the winter season, when the danger of epidemic disease was lower. Even then the public was aware that urban crowding during the warm summer months led to outbreaks of plague, dysentery, and other epidemics, and those who could afford it spent summers in the less densely populated countryside. The land-owning middle class built in a less lavish style, raising two- and three-story houses constructed of timber frame. The interior and exterior walls were built of plaster and clay over lathe construction, not so very different from the way plaster interior walls were made in the early 20th century, before gypsum dry wall was invented. Houses were roofed with tile, slate, or sometimes with straw thatch. The dominance of wood structures explains why London's Great Fire of 1666, a decade after Harvey's death, was so terrible.

In the Middle Ages, dramas were staged in open marketplaces by itinerant players, whose pay depended on passing a hat for voluntary contributions, or by church groups presenting morality plays and seasonal features, such as the Passion of Christ. In the second half of the 16th century, Queen Elizabeth I and other prominent members of the government sponsored troupes of players, who preferred to stage their plays in the homes of aristocrats or publicly at inns, where admission could be controlled and fees collected systematically.

In the last quarter of the 16th century, permanent theaters, buildings devoted to staging dramatic performances, were built in London's suburbs—the Theatre was established in 1576, the Curtin in 1577, and the Rose in 1587. They were just beyond reach of the moral censure of London's mayor and councilmen, who regarded the new players' groups with a measure of alarm. These theatres provided the physical and social setting for the emergence of bold, new plays with political and historical themes and biting social satire, penned by playwrights such as Christopher Marlowe and Shakespeare. The Globe, the theater Shakespeare was mainly associated with, was erected in 1598 from material taken from the old Theatre, which had been closed down and dismantled.

During Harvey's lifetime the theater as playhouse/stage became a metaphor for the world and the events that transpired in it. Indeed, the very word *theater*, which denotes a place for oratory and plays in antiquity, was commonly used in the 16th century as a title for a book of maps, an atlas, or "theater" of the known world. Conversely, when Shakespeare pronounced that "all the world's a stage" (*As You Like It*, act II, scene 7), he meant to point out the correspondences between the theater as playhouse and the world as a performance, in

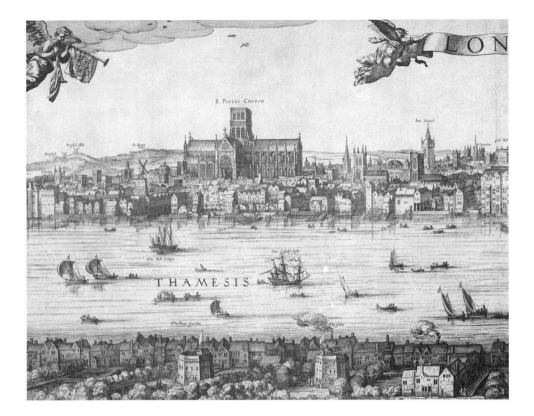

which every creature plays out its assigned role, which was provided by the omniscient creator of all things.

When Harvey, later in life, returned to England from Padua, Italy, English theater was quickly becoming fashionable in and around London. The new theater buildings mainly catered to the wealthy, who bought higher-priced tickets to sit in sheltered, raised galleries that faced the stage, but they also admitted ordinary folk, who paid little to stand in the open yard between the galleries and the stage. On occasion, Shakespeare addressed this motley, noisy crowd in some of his plays. Some of his bawdy and humorous comments, for example, seem targeted to the commoners in the audience.

The concept of the theater as a permanent building dedicated to dramatic performance began to emerge in this

text continues on page 22

Shakespeare staged many of his plays at the Globe theater in the foreground (right of the center). Across the Thames River, St. Paul's Cathedral dominates the city of London, where Harvey lived during his years as Lumley lecturer and physician at St. Bartholomew's Hospital.

I n William Shakespeare's tragedy *Henry IV,* the Earl of Westmoreland asks the Archbishop of York why he, normally a promoter of Christian peace, is leading an army in rebellion against King Henry, who gained the throne through the murder of his relative, King Richard. The archbishop responds:

> We are all diseased,
> And with our surfeiting and wanton hours
> Have brought ourselves into a burning fever,
> And we must bleed for it; of which disease
> Our late king, Richard, being infected, died.
> But, my most noble Lord of Westmoreland,
> I take not on me here as a physician,
> Nor do I as an enemy to peace
> Troop in the throngs of military;
> But rather show awhile like fearful war,
> To diet rank minds sick of happiness
> And purge the obstructions which begin to stop
> Our very veins of life.
> (part 2, act IV, sc. 1)

Shakespeare's audience would have readily understood: a surfeit (excess) of food and drink led to overproduction of some of the body's basic constituents, which determined the mixture of its primary qualities. These basic constituents were the four humors (fluids): blood, choler (yellow bile), phlegm, and melancholy (black bile). Each of the humors was associated with two of the primary qualities. Blood, for example, was hot and moist, whereas phlegm was cold and moist, choler was hot and dry, and melancholy was cold and dry. This medical system was so pervasive that vestiges of it remain today. We still refer to people who are by nature gloomy and rather subdued as "melancholic," though we no longer attribute the temperament to a mixture of humors that is rich in black bile. Similarly, the terms sanguine, phlegmatic, and choleric (or bilious) remain in modern use.

The accepted therapy for a fever, which is characterized by too much heat, was to bleed the patient by venesection (cutting into a vein) or by

According to Greek physicians Hippocrates and Galen, health and disease were governed by a mixture of four "humors," or basic fluids, in the body and its parts. The humor that was naturally dominant conveyed a particular "temperament" to the person. These temperaments are personified in a 14th-century manuscript (clockwise from top left) as phlegmatic (predominance of phlegm), sanguine (predominance of blood), melancholic (predominance of black bile), and choleric (predominance of yellow bile).

applying leeches to suck blood through the skin, or by making small incisions in the skin with a lancet and then placing a warmed glass over the wounds. As the air within the cupping glass cooled, the pressure dropped and sucked the blood into the glass from the body.

In Shakespeare's verse, the archbishop hopes that the obstructions of the veins that have resulted from surfeit can be "purged" by a threatening show of force rather than a bloodbath. Medically this was achieved by administering a drug (a purgative) to purge the excess humor or humors from the body through one orifice or another. Such a medicine might be a mixture of herbs or a drug made by a chemical procedure, for example, distilling oils, acids, or salts.

text continued from page 19

period. This development parallels the establishment of permanent facilities for public anatomical dissections of the sort that William Harvey attended and learned to perform.

At the end of the 16th century, the curriculum at the University of Cambridge was in large part still basically medieval. Harvey began by studying the liberal arts, which entailed learning rhetoric (the skill of writing and speaking effectively and persuasively), moral, political, and natural philosophy. Harvey learned these topics mostly from Aristotle's treatises and later commentaries upon them, but also from the writings of Cicero, Pliny, Plato, and other classical authorities. All well-educated scholars studied natural philosophy, which included a survey of arithmetic, geometry, and astronomy.

To prepare for advanced medical study, students also studied astronomy, and its relative astrology. The practice of medicine at that time involved the belief that health and disease depended on the seasons and "aspects," or spatial arrangements, of the planets in the sky. Particular alignments of planets and their appearance in certain signs of the zodiac were thought to have a direct correlation with the flow of fluids and the functions of the major organs in the body. Many physicians made a lucrative practice of casting horoscopes as part of their treatment of patients.

For the most part, however, natural philosophy comprised subjects that took their names from books written by Aristotle such as *Physics, On the Heavens, Meteorology, On the Soul* (psychology), *Metaphysics,* and *On Generation and Corruption.* These subject areas determined the questions that scholars asked, and framed the kinds of answers that were given. It may seem odd that a body of literature composed at the height of ancient Greek civilization should be given such prominence almost two millennia later, but Aristotle's inquiry was so all-encompassing and his work so methodical that it was not surpassed during the ensuing ages. This was especially true in the Latin-speaking world of Western Europe during the Early Middle Ages (approximately 400–1000 CE), where education—even basic literacy—suffered the disruption of repeated invasions and population migrations.

After Europeans rediscovered Aristotle's treatises in the 13th century, his ideas came to dominate basic university education and natural philosophy (science) in particular. This was still true in 1600, and Harvey assimilated Aristotle's view of the natural world as undergoing a continuous process of growth and decay, as objects moved from one state of existence to another.

Aristotle had been a student of the great idealist philosopher Plato, who taught that the world of sense experience was a poor imitation of the true reality, which consisted of perfect, immaterial ideas. Unlike his teacher, however, Aristotle was mainly interested in things; he was foremost a biologist, curious about the constantly changing world

Dutch artist Rembrandt's 1653 painting depicts Aristotle, the ancient Greek philosopher, dressed in 17th-century Dutch attire pondering a bust of Homer, the great epic poet and founder of Greek literature. Aristotle was widely revered as a founder of the Western philosophical tradition, and his teachings were the basis for university education during William Harvey's time.

around him and how its various parts came into existence and subsequently disappeared. Aristotle wrote on many philosophical subjects, from political theory to poetry, but when it came to natural philosophy, his emphasis was on what we might call the developmental, or living. For example, the ancients believed crystals and minerals to be growing and living. Early Europeans followed their predecessors in regarding minerals as organic, capable of growing and aging within the earth. Perhaps this idea was based on the observed "growth" of crystals. For this reason, Aristotle's teachings provided a good foundation for medical theory.

Although the content of the medieval arts curriculum—the subject matter that the student was required to master before being awarded a Bachelor of Arts (B.A.) degree—consisted largely of works by Aristotle and other ancient Greek and Roman writers, the manner of presenting and debating assertions about anything and everything was decidedly characteristic of the Middle Ages. It so dominated the universities that it was called simply "the scholastic method." According to the statutes laid down for Cambridge University in 1570, students were expected to attend two or three disputations per week from their second year and participate in them from their third year. Earning a B.A. degree required not only examinations, but also a public disputation on selected "theses," or philosophical assertions. Thus, a university education aimed to provide the student with knowledge and also with the ability to present and defend that knowledge.

After receiving the B.A. degree in the summer of 1597, William Harvey probably began to attend medical lectures at Cambridge University and focus his reading on medicine. The medical curriculum included studying the works of medieval medical writers, particularly Arabic authors in translation or commentaries on their works by medieval and Renaissance European medical writers. But the study of medicine was dominated by the ideas and practices of the

earliest comprehensive medical treatises, which were attributed to the legendary Hippocrates (who worked in Greece
in the 5th century BCE) and to the greatest classical medical
writer of them all, Galen of Pergamon (who worked in what
is now Turkey, then part of the Roman empire, as well as in
Rome itself, in the 2nd century CE).

Galen's enduring success rested on his ability to consider
the entire scope of medical and surgical practice of his day
and integrate it into a coherent medical theory that was based

The Persian philosopher and physician Avicenna's Book of the Whole Canon of Medicine *was originally written in Arabic. The* Canon *was translated into Latin and presented the fundamentals of the medicine of Hippocrates and Galen, shown seated to the left of Avicenna. It was the most widely used medical school textbook in late medieval Europe.*

on a thorough understanding of Aristotelian natural philosophy. His synthesis of practical medicine and natural philosophy proved to be very influential in the long run, becoming the foundation of medieval Arabic and subsequently European Christian medical education. Followers of this approach to medical knowledge and practice are called Galenists.

In ancient Greece and Rome, medicine was largely a craft, not an intellectual pursuit, but Galen's explanation of the workings of the body and the nature of health and disease in philosophical terms helped make it a legitimate philosophical field, worthy of a scholar. This groundwork bore fruit in the medieval universities, where academically trained physicians and medical authors sought to elevate medicine from its early medieval status as a craft to the level of an educated profession.

As the university system developed in the 13th century, four schools or departments, called "faculties," emerged: the arts faculty and graduate faculties in theology, law, and medicine. One consequence of this was that the majority of university-educated scientists in the early modern period (the 16th and 17th centuries) were trained in medicine. Another consequence was that they were imbued with the ideas and approaches of Aristotle and Galen. The most respected scientists of the 17th century—Galileo Galilei, Johannes Kepler, Isaac Newton, and William Harvey—all of them, whether trained in medicine or not, were steeped in this classical, Aristotelian tradition as students, although they eventually departed from it in the course of their careers. This common educational background permitted them to study and teach anywhere in Europe, and it allowed them to write in a language and dialectical style that ensured that they could be understood by any university-educated European. Therefore, when William Harvey left Cambridge University in the fall of 1599 and traveled to northern Italy to study medicine where there were several good medical schools, it was no great adjustment for him.

At the turn of the 17th century there was probably no better place to study academic medicine than at the University of Padua, located near Venice in northeastern Italy. There were other universities renowned for their medical teaching—Paris and Montpellier in France for example—but for clinical training and anatomy, the University of Padua was on the cutting edge.

At that time, Padua was a part of the Venetian Republic. This had several consequences. On the one hand, its affairs were dominated and controlled by Venice's powerful merchants and organized craftsmen; this limited both the city's and the university's autonomy. On the other hand, the Venetian Republic offered a degree of protection from the political machinations of the Vatican and the monarchies to the north and west, which made the university a fairly secure environment, by 16th-century standards, in an era wracked by religious wars.

This engraving shows the University of Padua in 1601, when Harvey was a student there. The circular anatomical theater, which still exists, is depicted in cross section on the left. The list below the picture identifies professors' scheduled classes for that year.

Already in the 14th century, medicine had been growing in prominence in the northern Italian town of Bologna, where a string of inspired and innovative teachers incorporated clinical observation and practice into the medical curriculum at the university. Attendance at an annual public anatomical dissection was mandated in the university statutes. This practice became widespread in Europe's medical schools in the following centuries. Medical students at Bologna did not learn medicine just by reading Aristotle and Galen and Hippocrates and the Arabic commentators, but also by visiting patients and, on occasion, exploring the internal architecture of the body through anatomical dissections and postmortem examinations, or autopsies. This tradition spread to the University of Padua, which was founded by teachers and students from Bologna. By the time William Harvey set foot in Padua, a long series of brilliant medical and surgical instructors had made the university famous for its medical education.

Perhaps the most famous of the 16th-century anatomists is Andreas Vesalius. He had come to University of Padua in 1537 to obtain an M.D. and was subsequently appointed professor of surgery. Vesalius had previously trained at the University of Paris, a leader in the study of Galen's treatises as written in the original Greek, and he was at the forefront in refining Galen's anatomical procedures. Vesalius's 1543 anatomy text, *On the Architecture of the Human Body,* was the first to use high-quality, naturalistic illustrations that were keyed to the text. Several brilliant anatomists succeeded him at Padua, including Gabriele Fallopio, famous for his study of reproductive anatomy, and Realdo Colombo, whose investigation of the valves of the heart led him to argue that blood passes from the right side of the heart to the left side through the lungs. Harvey's teacher Hieronymus Fabricius of Aquapendente, who is remembered for his careful study of the valves in the veins, succeeded Colombo. Thus, Harvey was the academic heir of Europe's finest anatomists.

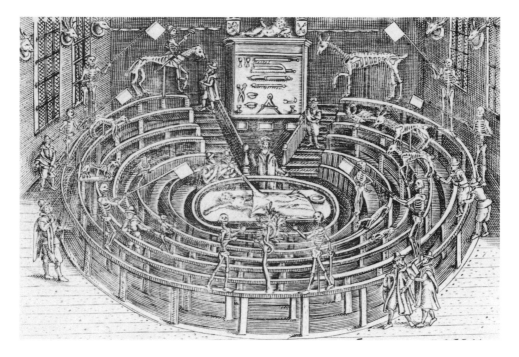

Part of the medical education at the University of Padua consisted of anatomical demonstrations set up on temporary stages. The increasing importance of anatomy and the frequency of anatomical demonstrations at the university must have made the repeated construction and removal of temporary anatomical stages irksome. To remedy this situation, Europe's first indoor anatomical theater was constructed at Padua in 1584. In 1594, not 20 years after London's first permanent drama theater, it was replaced by a permanent facility designed by Fabricius that was better suited for audiences. The historical coincidence of both kinds of theater suggests that the "witnessing" of dissections had a social function: the display of the inner body provided instructions to medical students, and the public dissections became a social event for the non-medical public. During Harvey's lifetime there were even occasions when admission was charged to the anatomical theater and prominent citizens who paid to witness these public spectacles would be seated closest to the dissection "stage."

This 1610 engraving of an anatomical theater at Leiden shows the theater as a kind of artistic and moral museum. When not used for public dissections, the skeletons of humans and animals that were employed to demonstrate anatomy were exhibited in the theater, with banners exhorting visitors to be mindful of life's brevity.

The themes that physical life is fleeting and death is arbitrary had captivated artists and moralists since the Black Death, the first great onslaught of epidemic bubonic plague in the middle of the 14th century. Epidemics of one sort or another, including bubonic plague, recurred every 10 or 20 years in most areas, and society had learned to live with periodic waves of disease that killed people without much regard for age, wealth, or righteousness. The result was a fascination with mortality and the human body. Seventeenth-century illustrations of anatomical theaters are often adorned with skeletons of humans and other animals, paying homage to the theme of the death of the flesh.

But witnessing dissections came to play another role, too. It certified the validity of observation. Anatomists who wished to assert a claim concerning an anatomical discovery knew that it would gain greater validity if their research was observed and proved by credible witnesses. Thus, the frontispiece of Vesalius's great anatomical treatise showed Vesalius dissecting a body in the presence of an audience. In the 17th century such "witnessing" played an important part in the creation of science based on an accepted body of facts. In fields of study where logical proofs were impossible to construct, physical demonstration and the creation of consensus replaced formal logical proof in producing a body of scientific facts upon which theories could be built. Harvey presented his scientific observations in a way that was reproducible, or in a way that convinced his readers that they were repeatable and had been witnessed—and therefore were reliable. This gave his work a lasting credibility and made it a model for modern scientific writing.

It is no accident that this method became a part of Harvey's scientific work; the tradition of Aristotelian research was especially strong at Padua, as was the experimentalism that it nurtured. Harvey's medical mentor Fabricius was affected by this "new" Aristotlian approach. Fabricius's research program aimed to learn the form and

The title page illustration from Andreas Vesalius's 1543 pioneering anatomical textbook, Seven Books on the Architecture of the Human Body *shows Vesalius demonstrating the anatomy of a female cadaver amid the pandemonium of a public dissection. Vesalius made a point of personally dissecting what he was teaching about, rather than the traditional method, where the lecturer read from an authoritative text while instructing a surgical assistant. Under the leadership of Vesalius and his successors, the University of Padua was renowned as a center for Europe's finest anatomical training.*

function of the parts of animal bodies. It was not defined by the established standard medical curriculum, which was intended to train healers rather than pursue general science. Paduan anatomists were not just physicians, but medical biologists, foremost among their European peers in the techniques of human dissection. This gave Harvey a perspective on the human body that was lacking in more tradition-bound universities.

From Fabricius and his younger colleague, Julius Casserius of Piacenza, Harvey learned how to dissect and vivisect animals. Vivisection, the experimental dissection of animals while they are still alive, is shocking to the modern sensibility, and throughout the ages scientists have expressed unease about intentionally bringing pain to animals. However, ancients medical researchers recognized vivisection as essential for learning about how living bodies function, as opposed to merely determining the nature of the dead shells of creatures. Sixteenth- and 17th-century "chemical" physicians, who made diagnoses based on chemical theories and prescribed medicines that were prepared by laboratory methods and traditional herbal remedies, persistently criticized the universities for their emphasis on human anatomy. They felt that dissecting cadavers revealed only the nature of dead bodies, and not the "vital philosophy" that characterized living systems. The key, of course, was to connect the dead bodies' structures to their living functions, but this was too often a matter of speculation and did not make the physician a better healer.

Vivisection had been practiced in ancient Alexandria (today Egypt), the heart of scientific activity in the Greco-Roman world. It was even reported that the medical researchers and teachers Herophilus and Erasistratus had vivisected human beings—condemned prisoners provided to them by the rulers of Greek Egypt—in the third century BCE. By Galen's day, vivisection had been abandoned for centuries and had become faint rumors of past immorality. However, Galen understood that advance in medical learning comes from a better knowledge of anatomy. He sought out a variety of animals for experiments, including the Barbary ape (a kind of ape that lives in northern Africa and southern Spain), which he recognized as very near to humans in form.

From vivisectional experiments Galen was able to fathom the functions of some of the nerves and provide enough observational information to venture some fairly elaborate physiological theories. Many of these theories turned out to be grossly erroneous, which can be explained in part by the limitations of his research, and in part by his mistaken interpretations of what he saw. In fact, his anatomical procedures were not much different from those William Harvey practiced in the 17th century, when the scientific achievements of antiquity were being repeated, renewed, and eventually surpassed. Harvey's genius was to combine Galen's methods, which had been refined and brought to a high level of skill by the Paduan anatomists, with a systematic inquiry into the function and purpose of the body's parts, modeled on the natural philosophy of Aristotle. Whereas Galen had dissected animals to learn about humans, Harvey dissected humans and other animals to learn about all animals. In this he was following both Aristotle and Fabricius, his mentor at the University of Padua. Studying at that particular university at that particular time in history provided Harvey with the background that enabled him to make a breakthrough in human physiology.

On April 25, 1602, William Harvey was granted the degree of *Medicinae Doctor.* It was less than a century after the churches of Northern Europe broke ties with the Roman Catholic church, and Protestants like Harvey were not permitted to receive the M.D. from the Catholic authorities in Italy; so the university set up a separate award ceremony at the palace of Count Sigismund, whose signature warranted Harvey's diploma on behalf of the Holy Roman Emperor, Rudolf II. Soon Harvey was on his way back to London, where he applied to become a candidate for membership to the Royal College of Physicians. He was initially refused.

The Royal College of Physicians was not a "college" in the sense of an undergraduate university, but a professional association very much like a craft guild. Its main purpose was to give the elite, university-educated physicians of

London complete control over who was allowed to practice the medical craft in and around the city. For 200 years after its founding in 1518, the College regulated the myriad doctors, surgeons, apothecaries, and other healers who plied their trades in the city. The College's censors made sure that medical practitioners were properly trained and licensed. They limited the surgeons to surgical practice and the apothecaries to making and dispensing drugs. And prosecuted and suppressed those who proffered medical services without the approval of the College. But almost from the beginning, the medical needs of the people and the willingness of countless immigrant physicians and homespun quacks, or fraudulent healers, to accommodate consumer demands overwhelmed the effectiveness of the College's censors. It was a long and losing battle to bring order to a medical world that could not yet adequately prove that scientific medicine was better than folk remedies.

William Harvey's M.D. diploma from the University of Padua is beautifully hand decorated.

In 1603, the year after Harvey returned to England, Queen Elizabeth I, whose long reign had brought a measure of stability and prosperity to England, passed away at the ripe old age of 69. She was succeeded by the son of her old Catholic adversary, Mary Queen of Scots, whom Elizabeth had ordered killed in 1587. Since Elizabeth had no children or living siblings, King James VI of Scotland was the most direct successor to the Crown and became James I of England. Although his mother and her family had been staunchly Catholic, James was very much a Protestant. His lively court, however, brought down the censure of the morally strict, puritan Calvinists (also called Puritans), whose growing power and demands Elizabeth had carefully balanced against the persistent influence of the English Catholics. The political and religious tensions that marked James's early rule foreshadowed the upheavals that cast a dark shadow over Harvey's later career.

The Royal College of Physicians was rebuilt after the Great Fire of London in 1666. During Harvey's lifetime the College was located on Amen Corner.

In the meantime, Harvey sought to establish his credibility as a London physician. The examiners of the College of Physicians had rejected his initial application for licensure, but they gave their tacit approval for him to practice medicine, perhaps because there was an outbreak of plague and practitioners of all sorts were needed. Whether he availed himself of this opportunity or not, he soon reapplied.

Harvey was finally admitted to the College of Physicians as a Candidate for Fellowship in 1604. This meant that he would be licensed by the College to practice medicine while he worked toward full membership as a fellow. That fall, with his future as a London physician more secure, he married Elizabeth Browne. Not much is known about Mrs. William Harvey. She was 24-years old when they married—William was 26—and she was the daughter of a royal physician, Sir Lancelot Browne. As a physician to the new king, Harvey's father-in-law was in a good position to further the young doctor's career. However, he failed in his attempt to secure an appointment for William as physician at the Tower of London, and he died soon afterwards, in 1605.

The Tower of London was notorious as a prison for high-ranking enemies of the Crown, and a position there would have provided Harvey with an

King James VI of Scotland ascended the throne of England as James I in 1603, after Queen Elizabeth died without a direct heir, thus uniting the two kingdoms into Great Britain.

opportunity to rub shoulders with some of the period's most powerful and interesting characters. The best known of these characters today was Sir Walter Raleigh, whose attempts to colonize Virginia foreshadowed England's development as an empire. He was a man of action in an age that valued such men. But he was also envied as Queen Elizabeth's former court favorite and feared as an atheist, like his friend, Christopher Marlowe. Mistrusted and disliked by King James, Raleigh was sent to the Tower in December 1603. He was joined there two years later by Henry Percy, the Ninth Earl of Northumberland, who was suspected of sympathy with the perpetrators of the Gunpowder Plot, the conspiracy by English Roman Catholics to blow up Parliament, King James I, his queen, and his oldest son on November 5, 1605.

Percy was known as the "Wizard Earl" because of his deep interest in the occult sciences, mainly astrology and alchemy, and during his lengthy imprisonment, he was permitted to build a library and laboratory and enjoy the company of fellow scholars. Among these were several of the most famous mathematicians and physicians of the time, including Thomas Harrior, who had introduced the American potato to England on his return from Raleigh's expedition to Virginia. Raleigh, who was himself interested in literature and science, also conferred with Percy and his visitors. In such company Harvey would hardly have suffered the plight of an ordinary prison physician. But the appointment was not to be.

In 1605, William's mother died in Folkestone, and his father moved to London, where most of the Harveys lived and had established a business. The Harvey brothers and their father were unusually close and supportive of each other's business activities and personal affairs. The family business prospered because of the increasing trade between England and the eastern Mediterranean. Two of the Harvey brothers, Eliab and Daniel, eventually bought several estates in and around London and helped to manage William's financial affairs. He resided with them in his later years, when he was out of political favor with the ruling authorities.

William Harvey's career advanced steadily during the decade that followed. In 1607 he became a full Fellow of the Royal College of Physicians, which made him a voting member of the organization. His responsibilities consisted of governing the College and carrying out its functions, which included examination of medical practitioners, admission of candidates, and prosecution of quacks. In addition to being a Fellow, in 1613, 1625, and 1629, he was elected one of the College's four censors, an officer in the College. He was charged with visiting London's apothecary shops and assessing the quality of their drugs. In December of 1627, he became one of the eight elect members of the College, who examined physicians to determine whether they had sufficient education and training to practice in London. The following year he became treasurer, and was reelected the next year. Harvey remained an active supporter of the College and its medical mission to the end of his life.

As a Fellow of the Royal College of Physicians, Harvey enjoyed higher social status, especially in the London area, and this increased his access to wealthy and powerful patients. Although little is known about his private practice, over the years he occasionally treated such dignitaries as the Lord Treasurer and the Lord Chancellor, and Francis Bacon, who later became famous as a visionary and philosopher of the new science of the 17th century. However, Harvey's income from treating patients privately must not have been sufficient, at least in his early years as a physician, because in 1609 he applied for the position of physician at London's St. Bartholomew's Hospital.

In the early 1600s, it was customary to hire a physician for a position before it became vacant, in part to ensure a smooth transition of service. Harvey did not have to wait long for an opening and a chance to learn the ropes. The hospital's physician died the summer that Harvey was hired.

He took over his duties at St. Bartholomew's Hospital immediately and was formally appointed that fall. His position required that he come to the hospital at least one day a week to advise and prescribe medicines to the patients, keeping records of all prescriptions. The position provided a residence, which was adjoined to the hospital, but it was occupied. Since he already lived conveniently close by, Harvey declined to use it and was later compensated with an increase in salary.

In England, elite medicine studied in the universities and practiced by physicians was professionally distinct from surgery, which was considered a craft and learned by apprenticeship. Physicians mainly concerned themselves with internal medicine, diagnosing disease and recommending treatment or adjusting patient's diet. Treatment of skin conditions, wounds, fractures, and other such "external" conditions was the surgeon's job.

Becoming a surgeon did not require mastering Latin or studying philosophy. Ordinary surgical practices at that time, such as letting blood from patients to relieve them of dangerous "surfeits," or excesses of blood, were often carried out by barbers, who joined with the surgeons in a craft union called the Barber-Surgeons' Company. Physicians and surgeons were constantly defending their own professions against the other—physicians seeking to prevent surgeons from prescribing medicines to be taken internally, and surgeons making sure that physicians did not engage in traditional surgical procedures.

It is unlikely, therefore, that Harvey's position as physician at St. Bartholomew's offered him many opportunities to undertake anatomical research, except when he was called upon to conduct an autopsy with the help of a surgeon. However, his appointment as an anatomical lecturer at the Royal College of Physicians gave him just the platform he needed to carry out systematic investigations of human and animal anatomy along the lines that he had learned at Padua.

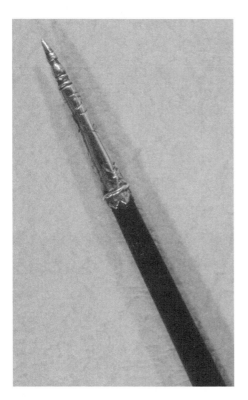

William Harvey is thought to have used this rod, made of whalebone and silver, to point out anatomical structures during his Lumley lectures at the Royal College of Physicians. These lectures were intended to acquaint London's surgeons with human anatomy, but they also helped Harvey reconceptualize the workings of the heart and vascular system.

In 1615 he was appointed Lumley Lecturer, a position he retained until 1656. The Lumley lectureship at the College of Physicians was named after Lord Lumley, who in 1581 established an ongoing series of surgical lectures to parallel those held at the Barber-Surgeons' Company. These lectures were intended for surgeons and physicians and they were held in both Latin and English, on Wednesday and Friday each week, from 10 to 11 A.M. The lectures covered topics in the basic surgical texts and surgical demonstrations on human cadavers accompanied the topics, for which the College had been granted permission to obtain up to four bodies a year. A surgeon was engaged as a prosector (one who "sects," or cuts)— an assistant who did the actual cutting—while the lecturer read the relevant passages in various texts concerning the parts being demonstrated. The whole course of lectures filled a six-year cycle, which was then repeated.

William Harvey was appointed to the Lumley lectureship about a year after the College of Physicians had moved into its new quarters at Amen Corner, not far from Harvey's residence. It is clear from the lecture notes that he compiled over the ensuing years that he used the lectures as a forum for general anatomical demonstrations as well as the required surgical ones, and as a means to undertake biological research like that conducted by Fabricius. Harvey was committed to the idea of showing his audience anatomical features whenever he could, rather than having them rely on written descriptions. This practice of building a body of facts on "ocular demonstrations," demonstrations that were performed before eye witnesses, rather than argued by logical deduction or on the basis of what was written in authoritative books, came to characterize English science during the second half of the 17th century.

Harvey started his first recorded lecture-demonstration on April 16, 1616. Over a three-day period, he dissected and lectured on the abdomen, the chest, and the head, following the traditional "three cavities" approach to anatomical demonstration. The order was very practical, since the tissues that were liable to decay most quickly were removed and examined first, which was very desirable in an age before artificial refrigeration. Even though much of Harvey's research at this point was devoted to examining the heart and the vascular system, only 9 of the 98 pages of his Lumley notes concern the heart, suggesting that he followed the requirements of the lectureship. Like his predecessors in Italy and elsewhere, he supplemented his human dissections with comparative anatomical demonstrations on lower animals. Harvey's use of comparative anatomical research was an important part of his program.

On February 3, 1618, William Harvey was appointed Extraordinary Physician to King James I, with a promise of advancement to Ordinary Physician when a position would become vacant. As Extraordinary Physician, Harvey did not have primary responsibility for the king or the royal family, but he would be consulted by the king's personal (ordinary) physicians on diagnosis and therapy. The appointment carried with it a further increase in professional status, and consequently a greater likelihood of being sought out by members of the aristocracy.

University-educated physicians like Harvey depended on aristocratic families and wealthy merchants, professionals, and shopkeepers for their livelihood and did what they could to market themselves to these classes. If they were especially lucky, they might find employment at the estates of the very wealthy landed gentry, for whom their employment was a symbol of power and prestige as well as

Surgeons used a wide variety of instruments in their craft, as depicted in this early German woodcut from the Strassburg surgeon Hieronymus Brunschwig's Book of Surgery, published in 1497. It shows tools for cutting, clamping, sawing, probing, drilling, and opening the flesh, vessels, and bones of the body. Instruments for salving, irrigating, fumigating, and injecting various smokes and fluids into the body's various orifices hang to the right and on the table.

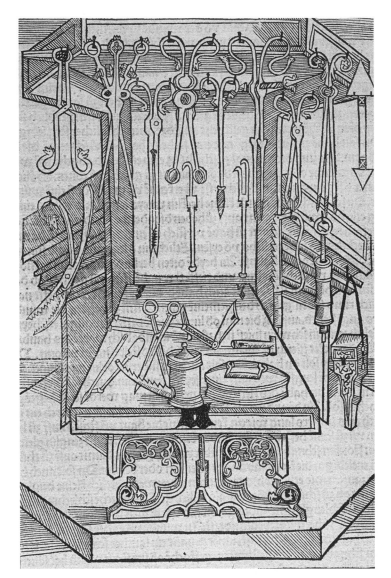

providing medical services. The medical elite also treated the less well to do, sometimes as municipal appointees, but often relied on their rich patrons to sustain their practice at a comfortable living standard. Being a royal physician also meant that Harvey belonged to the elite group of European royal physicians and that anything he might publish would therefore carry as much weight as something written by a medical professor.

William Harvey's adult life was devoted to his biological and medical studies, evident in his published works. Several other treatises, notebooks that contain material that he intended to use in his treaties, and personal letters disappeared during the course of the English Revolution and the Civil War. This partly explains the poverty of materials that would have permitted a better understanding of his personal life. He never had children, and the surviving records suggest that most of his energies were focused on his career and his membership in the Royal College of Physicians.

Harvey was a busy man in the decade that followed. He was a physician at St. Bartholomew's Hospital; an active member of the College of Physicians, where he also lectured twice a week; a consulting physician to the king; and he probably maintained some sort of private practice.

During this time he was eagerly investigating the nature of the heart and the vascular system, trying to make sense of certain features that the traditional medical theories did not adequately explain. He asked questions such as why the veins were larger nearer the heart, when they were thought to originate in the liver, or why the "vein" that served the lungs seemed much too large to be merely providing them nourishment and, moreover, had a structure more like an artery than a vein. The results of his investigations were finally published in 1628 and they dispelled forever the view of basic human physiology that had been handed down from Galen to the Renaissance.

EXERCITATIO
ANATOMICA DE
MOTV CORDIS ET SAN-
GVINIS IN ANIMALI-
BVS,

GVILIELMI HARVEI ANGLI,
Medici Regii, & Professoris Anatomiæ in Col-
legio Medicorum Londinensi.

FRANCOFVRTI,
Sumptibus GVILIELMI FITZERI.

ANNO M. DC. XXVIII.

The first edition of William Harvey's Anatomical Exercise on the Motion of the Heart and Blood in Animals *was published in Frankfurt, Germany, in 1628. English scholars at this time often chose to have their Latin-language scholarly works published in German or Swiss cities rather than in England because there were many skilled printers, fewer controls over what was published, and good access to European book markets.*

The Circulation of the Blood

William Harvey's monumental book, which established new directions for physiological research and forever changed the way the operations of the human body were conceived, was a rather small volume with one illustration and the unassuming title *Anatomical Exercise on the Motion of the Heart and Blood in Animals.* Published in 1628, it is considered to be one of the most important textbooks in the history of medicine and made Harvey familiar to most modern physicians as one of the pioneers of modern medicine. Yet his book is not about medicine as it was conceived in the 17th century, which would encompass study of the parts of the body, the diseases that afflict us, and the methods of treatment that aim to restore and maintain our health. It is not even about human anatomy the way it was taught then, that is, the study of the locations, shapes, and presumed uses of the various major organs. It is instead an extended series of propositions and observations about the operation of one particular organ, the heart, and the vessels connected to it.

Since Harvey's time we have come to think of the cardiovascular system as one unified system, but in the early 17th century it was still viewed the way the ancient Greeks had viewed it—as a group of separate organs and systems, each with its own independent function. The venous system was believed to transport blood from the liver to the rest of the body, including the heart, in order to provide it with nutrition. The arterial system was thought to transport blood that had been refined in the heart and endowed with some sort of vitality, either vital heat or some kind of spirit that gave energy to the body. The heart was seen to serve two functions: the right side received a portion of the blood from the veins and furthered it to the lungs for their nourishment; the left side heated blood that it received through the wall separating the two halves (the cardiac septum). It was considered a possibility that a small amount of blood also came to the left ventricle from the lungs, but their main function was thought to provide air to moderate the natural heat in the left ventricle and prevent it from overheating the blood.

Anatomists in ancient Alexandria, Egypt, determined that the human heart consists of two roughly symmetrical halves, right and left, that were equipped with valves (1,2,3,4) to force fluid and spirit (pneuma) to flow in a directional pattern.

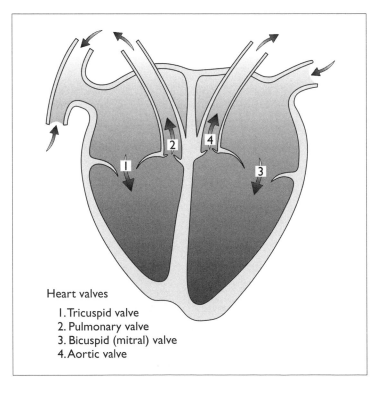

Heart valves

1. Tricuspid valve
2. Pulmonary valve
3. Bicuspid (mitral) valve
4. Aortic valve

A proper amount of heat was considered a necessary condition for health and therefore was of great concern to physicians. Too little heat was a sign of weakness and decline (old people were regarded as deficient in heat and moisture), and too much heat (fever) could overcome the body. Patients with fevers were often bled, in part to cool them, and weak patients were given "cordials," which warmed and fortified the heart (the *cor* in "cordial" means "heart" in Latin). The lungs were regarded as ventilators, whose principal function was to cool the heart and perhaps also to provide it with vital spirit or air, which would then be mixed with the blood in the left ventricle.

Harvey singled out these four basic parts of the body for study and argued that they worked together for one purpose: the circulation of the blood. His book is not a medical textbook, but rather what we might call a scientific monograph: a philosophical inquiry into the operation of one aspect of animal physiology. This distinction is not important today, when we hardly blink at the wide variety of kinds and disciplines of pure research that are part of modern medicine, but in early modern Europe, medicine and natural philosophy were still distinct disciplines.

Even though Harvey was a royal physician, a member of the College of Physicians, and a lecturer in anatomy, his book was regarded as a philosophical treatise. Although it was admittedly important for medical scholars, the book was addressed mainly to those who were interested in philosophical issues and not strictly medical ones. This distinction was a reflection of the teaching traditions at the universities, where medicine was dominated by the teachings of Galen, and natural philosophy depended on the works of Aristotle and the commentaries based on them. In practice, however, medicine and philosophy were tightly bound.

This was partly the legacy of Galen, who realized that healing would remain an inferior craft unless it was integrated with philosophical theory and therefore became an intellectual pursuit as well. Medieval physicians realized the same thing and made medicine an academic field and a part of the university curriculum by requiring students to study Aristotelian philosophy before they studied medicine as a graduate subject. But the two fields of study persisted as distinct disciplines: medicine was about the health and healing of humans, whereas natural philosophy was about the organization, operation, and purpose of the natural world, and included anatomy and physiology only insofar as the human body was part of nature. Harvey's book fell within the second category.

Anatomical Exercise on the Motion of the Heart and Blood is a carefully structured argument—exactly what one might expect from somebody trained in academic declamation and disputation, but with an important difference. Harvey frequently explains experimental procedures in a way that invites the reader to reconstruct them in the mind or perhaps to perform them. Unlike the most widely used medieval and early modern surgical and anatomical textbooks, which contain elaborate illustrations of the shape, location, and position of the parts of the body, Harvey's book contains only one illustration that features a set of four related figures.

This absence of pictures was probably a deliberate choice, reflecting Harvey's commitment to experimental method. He felt that knowledge obtained by direct, personal observation had a level of certainty that was greater than reasoned speculation. Here he was following Aristotle's research method, as presented in his books on the classification and investigation of animals, which Harvey had carefully studied at the University of Padua. The reader, by actually recreating Harvey's experiments or by "virtually" witnessing them in the mind's eye, was forced to follow each step of Harvey's method specifically, in a way that a general examination of illustrations did not require.

One might well wonder, then, why Harvey included the one illustration that he did. Its four figures depict a simple but persuasive experiment that can be performed on a human arm without dissection or vivisection. The experiment involves tying a tourniquet around the arm above the elbow and adjusting the tightness to demonstrate that the blood can be either cut off from the arm or permitted to overfill the arm, causing the veins to bulge. This was the same procedure used by physicians and surgeons to prepare a patient for bloodletting; the removal of blood from a vein

One of the most common therapies of early medicine was the letting of blood by cutting into a vein, called venesection, or phlebotomy. Blood could be let from many places on the body, depending on the particular ailment, but the veins near the elbow were commonly used. Often the work was done by a surgeon or barber-surgeon, shown here with his apprentice.

in the arm was a common treatment for a variety of medical conditions and was even recommended as a means of preventing disease.

By using this diagram, Harvey was quietly appealing to the common experiences of every physician and probably of most patients, too. This feature of Harvey's book, his appeal to direct observation and personal experience, ensured that his ideas would not be dismissed until they had been tried and retried across Europe, and made it one of the foundation texts for a profound change in the way science was conducted. His use of experimentation foreshadowed what was to become a cornerstone of the "new science." This method was practiced at the Royal Society in London and the Royal Academy of Sciences in Paris in the 1660s, and at a host of similar scientific societies that sprang up in Europe's intellectual capitals during the Age of Enlightenment between the years 1690–1790.

Anatomical Exercise on the Motion of the Heart and Blood in Animals contains 17 chapters, most of which are quite short. The first seven introduce Harvey's topic and focus on the operation of the heart and the movement of blood into and out of the heart. Harvey does not provide the main arguments for the circulation theory until the second half of the book, beginning with chapter eight, which reads almost like a new introduction. This feature of the book has led medical historians to suspect that Harvey actually began writing the first part of the book before he had conceived that the blood circulates through the body. He may have realized this in the course of his research on the heart, either by reflecting on the design of the valves of the veins or in contemplating the amount of blood that must leave the heart with each beat. However, the organization of the book can also be explained as a logical way to construct an academic disputation or exercise, namely by first establishing the structure and action of the heart and then proceeding to demonstrate its use or function.

Fabricius had studied the action and use of the various parts of the body. He aimed to correct what he considered an overemphasis on the location, position, and shape of the organs, and consequent neglect of how they operated by his predecessors. Harvey's research method into the heart and blood vessels was a continuation of Fabricius' research program and aimed to study the heart's function in relation to the animal as a whole, not solely the position and characteristics of human organs. Harvey sought to determine how the heart and the blood vessels functioned by means of comparative anatomy and vivisection, and he was strongly influenced by Aristotle's thinking that the function of a part should be in agreement with its structure, a point that Fabricius had emphasized, too.

Harvey begins his book by drawing the reader's attention to various incongruities in previous physiological explanations of the heart, lungs, and blood vessels. If the arteries and veins truly constitute separate systems with different functions, why do they have a similar appearance in

This recreation of an illustration from Thomas Bartholin's Reformed Anatomy published in 1651 shows Galen's interpretation of the operation of the heart: (1) The left diagram shows the blood entering the right side of the heart from the vena cava (D) and (2) passing out to the lungs via valve K. (3) A small quantity of blood passes through the septum to the left side of the heart. (4) There it is mixed with air coming in from the lungs (right diagram), and then (5) it goes out through a valve into the aorta (F) to the body.

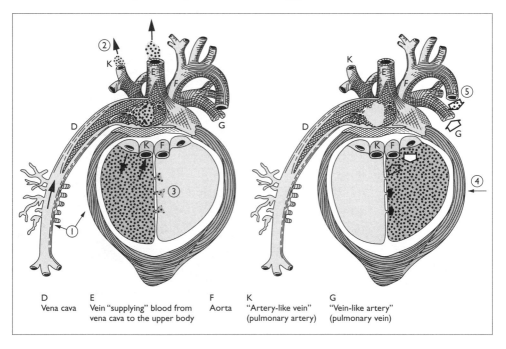

D	E	F	K	G
Vena cava	Vein "supplying" blood from vena cava to the upper body	Aorta	"Artery-like vein" (pulmonary artery)	"Vein-like artery" (pulmonary vein)

their smallest branches? Since the left and right halves, or ventricles, of the heart are similarly constructed, why do they differ radically in function? The Galenists taught that the right side of the heart received blood from the liver, sent a portion further to nourish the lungs, and its valves ensured that the blood going to the lungs did not flow back into the heart. The valves in the left side of the heart were presumably there to prevent air from returning to the lungs while permitting some type of smoky exhaust vapors—waste products from the generation of heat in the heart—to leak through and be expelled via the lungs.

Harvey raised various questions about these explanations. How can the heart valves prevent a reflux of spirits and yet not hinder the back flow of waste fumes? Moreover, if the pulmonary vein is for transporting air and fumes between the lungs and the left heart, why does one only find blood in it? Even Galen had been clear about that: his vivisection on a dog showed that even though its lungs were full of air, only blood could be observed in the pulmonary vein. This vein looks like a blood vessel, so why should it convey air? The valves in the left heart are similar to the valves in the right, so why should their functions differ? Likewise, pulmonary veins, which connect the lungs to the left side of the heart, and pulmonary arteries, which connect the lungs to the right side, are similar in size. This is not consistent with their supposed radically different functions—the pulmonary veins transporting air and the pulmonary arteries serving to nourish the lungs. Furthermore, why is the pulmonary artery so large, if it only feeds the lungs? And why would it need a whole ventricle for this purpose, when the rest of the body takes its nourishment directly from the veins?

Harvey assumed in all these cases that different functions should reflect different structural forms. He raised objections to Galen's claim that blood normally seeps through invisible pores between the two ventricles rather

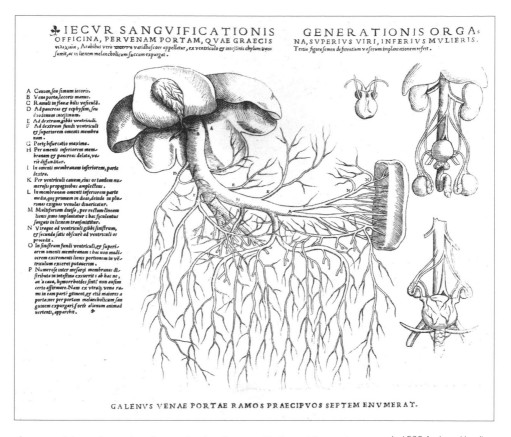

♣ IECVR SANGVIFICATIONIS OFFICINA, PER VENAM PORTAM, QVAE GRAECIS πυλχριδαι, Arabibus vero ουτουτη varidhas coer appellatur, ex ventriculo & intestinis chylum trans sumit, ac in lienem melancholicum succum expurgat.

GENERATIONIS ORGA- NA, SVPERIVS VIRI, INFERIVS MVLIERIS. Tertia figura semen de ferentium v aforum implantationem refert.

A Cauum, seu simum iecoris.
B Vena porta, iecoris manus.
C Ramuli in flaue bilis vesiculã.
D Ad pancreas & ecphysim, seu duodenum intestinum.
E Ad dextrum gibbi ventriculi.
F Ad dextrum fundi ventriculi & superiorem omenti membra nam.
G Portę bifurcatio maxima.
H Per omenti inferiorem mem branam & pancreas delata, va rie diffunditur.
I In omenti membranam inferiorem, parte dextra.
K Per ventriculi cauum, eius os tandem nu merosis propaginibus amplectens.
L In membranam omenti inferiorem parte media, quę primum in duas, deinde in plu rimas exiguas venulas diuaricatur.
M Multifariam diuisę, per rectam lineam lienis simo implantatur : hac fęculentus sanguis in lienem transmittitur.
N Vtraque ad ventriculi gibbi sinistrum, & secunda satis obscurè ad ventriculi os procedit.
O In sinistrum fundi ventriculi, & superi orem omenti membranam : hac non medi ocrem excrementi lienis portionem in vĕ triculum excerni putauerim.
P Numerose inter mesarę membranas di stributæ in intestina excurrit : ab hac ne, an a caua, hęmorrhoides sint? non ausim certo affirmare. Nam ex vtraę vena ra mi in eam parte ptinent, & etiã maiores a porta : nec per portam melancholicum san guinem expurgari, fortè alienum animad uertenti, apparebit. ♣

GALENVS VENAE PORTAE RAMOS PRAECIPVOS SEPTEM ENVMERAT.

than making the trip through the lungs. It is evident that both ventricles of the heart expand and contract at the same time, whatever the cause. Why, then, would blood be encouraged to leave one side and go to the other, if both sides are expanding? Harvey concluded that there were so many unanswered questions that a general investigation of the heart and blood vessels was warranted.

This approach of carefully correlating structural forms of parts with their functions was wholly in keeping with the research program of Aristotle and Galen that had fallen out of practice in intervening ages. In the first seven chapters of his book, Harvey also asserts that the blood found in the arteries is not intrinsically different from the blood found in the veins; that the blood naturally flows from the veins to the right heart; that blood passes from the right

In 1538 Andreas Vesalius published six anatomical illustrations. This one shows the portal vein, which Galen thought conveyed digested nutrients from the intestines to the liver (upper left), where it would be made into blood. Vesalius knew Galen had erroneously described the human liver as having five main lobes, but Vesalius's loyal portrayal of Galen physiological theo- ry, even though he knew better, is testimony to the authority credited to Galen.

heart into the left heart via the lungs; and that the heart forcefully contracts and presses blood into the arteries in the phase called "systole." When the heart's ventricles contract, they produce the main rise in arterial blood pressure that is measured in a modern physician's office as "systolic blood pressure." The secondary rise is called "diastolic blood pressure," and is caused by the contraction of the two small chambers that sit atop the ventricles (called "auricles"), which then causes the ventricles to fill with blood and expand (the phase called "diastole"). Harvey's account is modern in this regard, but in the 17th century these aspects of the heart's motion were not generally obvious.

Prior to Harvey's discoveries it was assumed that the more forceful movement of the heart was its expansion (diastole), and that the heartbeat was caused by the heart striking against the chest when it expanded. Since the heartbeat coincides with the pulse, it was supposed that the cardiac diastole coincided with the diastole of the arteries, meaning that the heart and arteries expanded at the same time, as one system. Harvey demonstrated that the heart is a muscle and contracts like a muscle; that the tip of it rises up and strikes the ribs when the heart itself is becoming hard and contracted (systole), expelling the blood into the arteries; and that the arteries then expand as the heart contracts. He noted that if you cut out the heart of an eel, you can watch it beat for hours and clearly see that it forcefully contracts and expands again as it relaxes. Harvey's use of cold-blooded animals, whose hearts move more slowly and are therefore easier to observe than the hearts of warm-blooded animals, is just one of the many instances in which comparative anatomy proved advantageous.

Explaining the flow of blood through the veins to the heart was another problem. One might accept an analogy between the heart as a muscle and a mechanical water pump, and indeed Harvey later made such an analogy explicit. But why would blood flow toward the heart through the veins when there was nothing to impel it? Harvey anticipated this question and argued that as we move around our muscles help to squeeze blood from the smaller veins to the larger ones and eventually move it toward the heart. Furthermore, although Harvey did not accept the Galenic idea that the heart had a natural faculty, or power, of attraction, he claimed that blood naturally moved toward its proper center (the heart) and had to be forced away from it, toward the extremities.

This kind of philosophical explanation seems incredible today, but was still commonplace in Harvey's time.

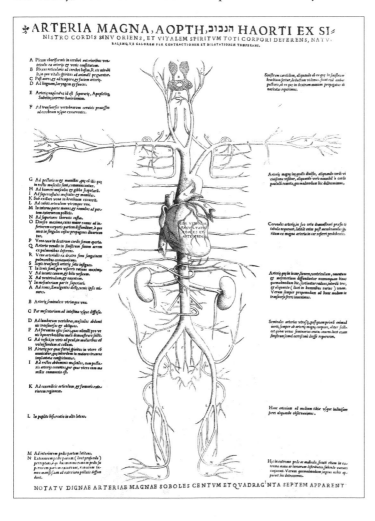

This illustration from Vesalius' 1538 series shows the arterial system and its chief organ, the heart. A portion of the vena cava is shown connected to the right side of the heart. The group of arteries in the head, called the rete mirabile, was supposed to supply the brain with blood, which was then filtered and endowed with "animal" spirit. Vesalius later showed that this structure was absent in humans, but in order to teach Galenic physiology, it was necessary to include it.

Another illustration from Vesalius's 1538 series shows the venous system and its chief organ, the five-lobed liver. The large vena cava (hollow vein) coming out of the top of the liver supplied blood to the heart, which connected at the oval opening (above the liver), as well as to the rest of the body.

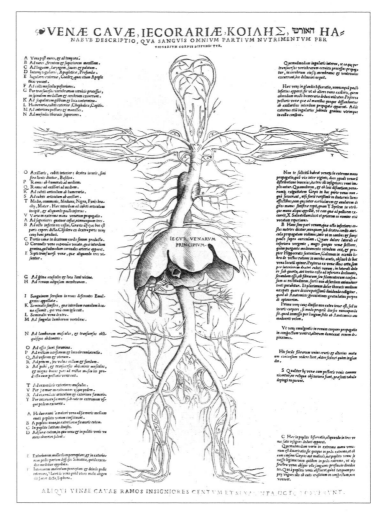

Perhaps the most common example was Aristotle's widely accepted argument that heavy objects fell "downward" because they naturally moved toward the center of the universe, which Aristotle believed was at the center of the earth. According to Aristotle, Earth, being heavy, naturally lay at the center of the universe. It was a consistent theory and had been taken for granted to be true.

In late antiquity, when Galen lived (2nd century CE), human dissection was not commonly practiced, probably because of social and religious attitudes about violating the bodies of the dead. Galen obtained limited knowledge of internal anatomy through his work as a surgeon, but most of his knowledge came from treatises written by his predecessors, anatomists who had worked at the museum and library at Alexandria (in Greek-ruled Egypt) several centuries earlier. He also dissected and occasionally vivisected other types of animals—dogs, sheep, pigs—and even apes which outwardly resemble humans. Vesalius and his contemporaries had already noted that Galen had erred in certain anatomical details because of his reliance on animals as models of human anatomy, and they aimed to correct those mistakes through careful dissection of humans.

Harvey used the results of research that he conducted on animals of all kinds. His research aimed not to find animals that resembled humans, but to study all kinds of ani-

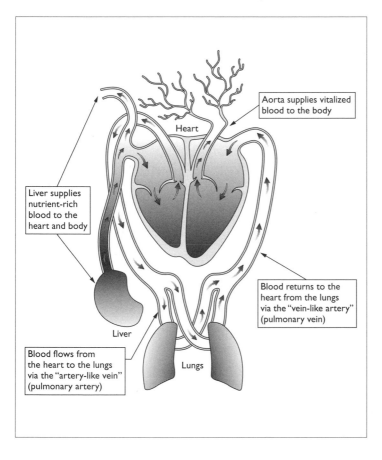

Aorta supplies vitalized blood to the body

Heart

Liver supplies nutrient-rich blood to the heart and body

Blood returns to the heart from the lungs via the "vein-like artery" (pulmonary vein)

Liver

Blood flows from the heart to the lungs via the "artery-like vein" (pulmonary artery)

Lungs

The diagram illustrates the pulmonary transit of the blood, described by anatomist Realdo Colombo in 1559. Blood manufactured in the liver is attracted to the right side of the heart, where the valves direct it through the lungs and into the left side of the heart. From there it is directed into the body. Harvey later theorized that the blood returns from the arteries into the veins, completing the circuit.

mals to learn how the heart functioned as a generic organ. He was exceptional in his investigation of fish and eels and even very small animals such as shrimp and insects, which he examined through a magnifying glass. He determined that they, too, had a heart, even if it was slightly different in form from that of more complex animals.

Harvey made good use of simpler forms of animals to establish the "pulmonary transit," or flow of blood from the right (venous) side of the heart to the left (arterial) side through the lungs. This was not a new idea, but it was essential to Harvey's full argument—which he would make in later chapters of his book—that the blood continually circulates through the body from the veins to the arteries and back to the veins. For Harvey, the placement and structure of the heart's valves dictated that the blood could do nothing else, since the valves into and out of the right ventricle, if truly fluid-tight, ensure that the blood leaves the right side of the heart and enters the lungs via the pulmonary artery.

The fact that arteries and veins were physically different was established before Galen, by the researchers in Alexandria. Arteries, especially the larger ones nearest the heart, are distinguished from veins on the basis of their extra layer of covering, which helps them withstand the higher blood pressure as the heart forces blood into them. But the fact that the pulmonary artery was attached to the right side of the heart, which is connected to the network of veins, led anatomists to consider it to be a vein that looked like an artery, and they called it the "artery-like vein." It was not until after Harvey's discovery that the term "pulmonary artery" was invented. Conversely, the vein that connects the lungs to the left side of the heart, which we call today the pulmonary vein, has the structure of a vein but is on the "arterial" (left) side of the heart, and was called the "vein-like artery." Finally, the valves between the left auricle and the left ventricle and at the exit of the left ventricle into the large main artery, the aorta, require that the blood move away from the lungs and into the arterial system, if they are fluid–tight.

Citing Galen, Harvey concluded that all valves enforce a flow in one direction, and considering the way that the valves of the heart are facing, this flow must be through the lungs from the right ventricle to the left auricle. He argued that the lung tissue is permeable and that the pressure exerted by the right ventricle, which serves only to impel blood into the lungs, assists the straining of the blood through the lungs. Galen had argued that nutrient was strained through the liver to be made into blood, and it was also believed that the kidneys strained wastes out of the blood. This provided ample precedent to regard organs as porous, that is filled with pores and therefore permeable. Furthermore, the pressure exerted by the pulsing right ventricle explained why the attached "artery–like vein" (the pulmonary artery) has the structure of an artery and why it pulses in time with the arteries.

Harvey also used information that he had obtained from his study of human development and his observations of children who were born dead, women who died during pregnancy, and fetuses that were aborted naturally. Such cadavers were often obtained from hospitals, such as the Hospital of St. Francis, or even St. Bartholomew's Hospital, where Harvey examined the deceased bodies of patients that no one claimed. Autopsies were also performed in the hospitals to determine the cause of death, and these examinations gave physicians and surgeons opportunities to observe the insides of human bodies. The location of St. Bartholomew's Hospital was near the streets where London's prostitutes lived and worked, and it may explain Harvey's access to bodies of women who died in childbirth or while giving birth to stillborn fetuses. These women were often without economic means or family to support them and they relied on the services of the hospitals during their pregnancy.

It was commonly known that in fetuses there are passages in the heart that normally grow closed as the child matures. The *foramen ovale* ("oval door") in the heart and the *ductus arteriosus* ("arterial duct") permit blood to pass from the right side of the heart into the aorta without going through the lungs. Harvey argued that this was because before a child is born, blood does not need to go through the lungs. With the bypass openings, the two ventricles of the fetal heart work as one—human embryos are in this regard like fish and other lungless animals, which have only a three-chambered heart.

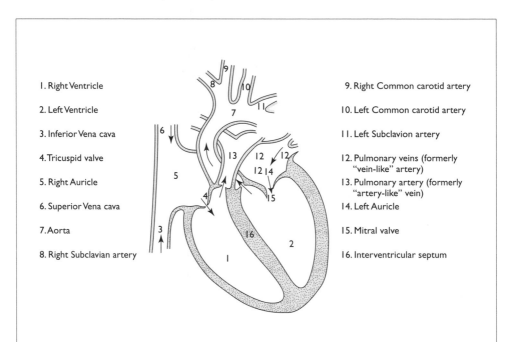

1. Right Ventricle

2. Left Ventricle

3. Inferior Vena cava

4. Tricuspid valve

5. Right Auricle

6. Superior Vena cava

7. Aorta

8. Right Subclavian artery

9. Right Common carotid artery

10. Left Common carotid artery

11. Left Subclavion artery

12. Pulmonary veins (formerly "vein-like" artery)

13. Pulmonary artery (formerly "artery-like" vein)

14. Left Auricle

15. Mitral valve

16. Interventricular septum

Harvey understood the blood to flow through the heart much as we do today. During the phase of the heart's activity called systole, the main part of the heart contracts, forcefully expelling the blood contained in the right ventricle (1) out through the pulmonary artery (13) to the lungs, and that contained in the left ventricle (2) out through the aorta (7) to the body's arterial system. When this happens, valves leading into the ventricles from the auricles (5, 14) are forced shut and prevent the blood from flowing backwards into the vena cava (3, 6) and pulmonary veins (12). The sharp rise in arterial blood pressure encourages the blood to flow out into the smallest arteries and into the tissues, where it makes its way into the veins. As the heart relaxes, the auricles (5, 14) fill with blood and then contract to fill the ventricles (1, 2) again (diastole).

Thus far, Harvey's book presented little if anything that had not been mentioned in previous medical literature. But in the eighth chapter he introduced a new idea: that the blood continually and normally circulates through the body. He claimed to have come to this realization while contemplating the sheer volume of blood that must be making the pulmonary transit with every beat. Where would all this blood go? Where could it all have come from? These questions, along with a rough calculation of the rate at which blood must be leaving the heart, formed the basis of his argument for circulation.

Harvey laid the groundwork for his theory of circulation by defining the veins and arteries not as separate systems serving different physiological functions, but as vessels that move the blood toward the heart and away from the heart, respectively. This deceptively simple step requires the reader to approach the argument on Harvey's terms: once the direction of blood flow was established as necessary, the rest of the argument became a matter of explaining why this should be.

In chapter nine Harvey set out three propositions that follow logically from this premise and concern what we might call the "economics" of the blood flow. First, the direction and flow of blood requires that blood passing through the heart must be generated from nutriment, or digested food, unless it is coming from somewhere else because it cannot flow backward into the venous system. Second, the blood that flows out of the heart must be used up by the body, unless it is going somewhere else because it cannot flow back to the heart through the arteries. Finally, the veins must continually drain blood from the body's parts and fill the heart because the blood cannot flow away from the heart toward the rest of the body through the veins.

In order to strengthen the first two points, Harvey offered a rough and very conservative calculation of how much blood must leave the heart (and therefore enter it from the veins) with each heartbeat. He framed his argument as a thought experiment, in which the reader imagines the steps, but it is clear from his words that it is based on his own physical experiments. "Let us suppose how much blood the left ventricle contains in its dilation," he wrote. "I have found in a dead man above two ounces." To make his argument, Harvey estimated that the left ventricle can hold somewhere between one-and-a-half and three ounces. The exact number does not matter to his argument. What matters is the general magnitude of the flow.

Taking into consideration that not all of the ventricle's contents are expelled in one contraction, Harvey offhandedly, but not unreasonably, guessed that at least an eighth or perhaps a quarter is ejected—therefore at least one dram (an eighth of an ounce) at each beat. Accordingly, if the heart makes a thousand, two thousand, three thousand, even four thousand beats in half an hour, more blood leaves the heart and enters the arteries than can be found in the entire body at any one time. It is all guesswork, but not baseless—"for I have tried it in a sheep," he wrote. Clearly, this amount of blood cannot be manufactured fast enough from what we eat to supply the heart, nor can it be used up that quickly for the body's nutrition. The logical consequence, according to Harvey, is that the blood must be going somewhere that does not entail its destruction, and coming from somewhere that does not require its manufacture. In other words, it must be recirculated.

Having presented a strong argument for the circulation of blood, Harvey now needed to describe how it circulates directionally—to demonstrate its path though the body. It is this demonstration that calls forth Harvey's best experimental evidence, which usually takes the form of various "ligature" experiments, in which one or more vessels are ligated, or tied shut, at places selected to demonstrate the direction of the blood flow. For example, Harvey writes that if in a

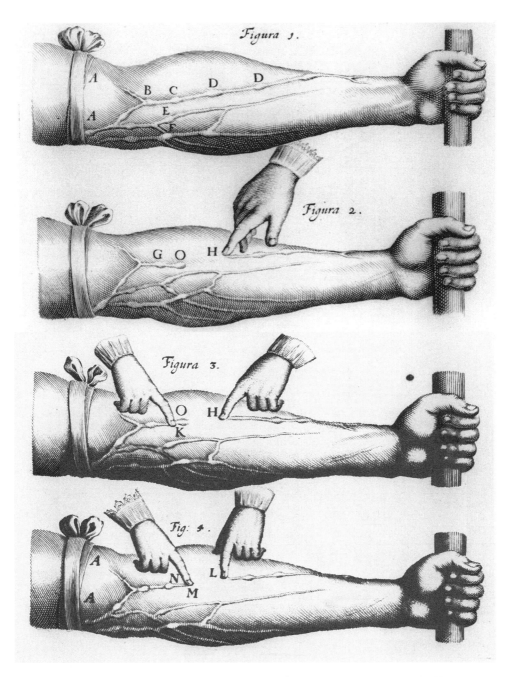

The four figures of this illustration accompany Harvey's explanation of a tourniquet experiment to show that blood enters the arm by way of the arteries and exits by way of the veins. This is the only illustration in his pioneering book, Anatomical Exercise on the Motion of the Heart and Blood in Animals. *It shows a procedure that would have been familiar to any physician or surgeon who let blood from the arm, implying that the experiment could easily be repeated.*

living animal you tie off the large vein near the heart, so that blood cannot enter the heart, and then open an artery, you will observe that the arterial system (and the lungs) will empty of blood, but the veins will not.

The ancient Greek anatomists had assumed the existence of hypothetical connections between the veins and the arteries, which they called *anastomoses*, and which were normally closed, but could open to permit blood to flow from one system to the other when the arteries were damaged externally. This explained why a person could bleed to death from a serious wound to either an artery or vein, yet the dissection of a cadaver that had died of natural causes would reveal clotted blood in the veins but little in the arteries. The latter observation had led the ancient anatomists before Galen to suppose that the veins normally carried only blood, and the arteries only air, but that blood would rush into them if they were punctured and the air permitted to escape. Galen had successfully demonstrated that this was not true, but he did not conclude that arteries contained only blood, or even the same kind of blood that the veins did.

Harvey's experiment was proof that blood cannot go "backward" through the veins and into the arteries—through the anastomoses—but must drain toward the heart. As for why the arteries of cadavers were usually devoid of blood, Harvey speculated that in natural death the lungs collapse before the heart stops beating, and they block the pulmonary transit, permitting the blood in the arteries to be pumped into the veins, but not allowing more blood into the arteries. As further support of his first proposition, Harvey introduced another experiment: Tying off the large vein a small ways from the heart of a living animal resulted in the space between the ligature and the heart emptying of blood and proved that the blood flows into the heart from the veins.

Harvey demonstrated that the blood in the veins came from the arteries by referring the reader to his experiment with a tourniquet on a man's arm. By tightening the tourniquet a great deal, he was able to stop nearly all blood flow into or out of the arm, as surgeons do before amputating a limb. Then, when the tourniquet was loosened a little, the arm filled with blood to the point of swelling up. Physicians and surgeons routinely followed this procedure prior to opening a vein to relieve the patient of "excess" blood. The traditional explanation for why this worked was that the veins, being discomforted by the tourniquet, attracted blood from the body, causing the arm to swell. Harvey argued that this might well account for why blood would be attracted to the arm, but it did not explain why more blood than the veins normally contain would be attracted and therefore cause swelling. This swelling, Harvey argued, was caused not by attraction, but by pressure—pressure created by the heart as it fills the veins. This demonstrated decisively that the veins could be filled *only* from the arteries.

Harvey appealed to physicians' familiarity with the tourniquet procedure for bleeding. He explained that when a tourniquet is very tight, it compresses both the arteries and the veins and completely blocks blood flow to and from the arm, and when it is loosened just enough, the blood is permitted into the arm but cannot leave. Logically, the blood must be entering through the deeper-lying arteries, and unable to leave through the veins. Physicians' experience with opening a vein for bleeding also showed that blood comes out of the vein on the far (extremity) side of the tourniquet. This strongly suggests that the blood is flowing from the extremities, where it could only have arrived by coming through the arteries.

To prove his third proposition about circulation, that the veins drain the body by permitting flow only toward the heart, Harvey needed to establish that the valves that anatomists had found in certain veins serve to prevent flow away from the heart. Fabricius had discovered or rediscovered these structures, but believed that they function as doors

This illustration in the 1603 book On the Little Doors of the Veins *by Harvey's teacher, Hieronymus Fabricius of Aquapendente, shows valves in the veins of the human leg. Fabricius thought that the valves regulated blood flow much like doors in an irrigation system, and in 1597 gave a public demonstration of this idea. Harvey, however, correctly understood that the valves regulate the direction of flow, not the rate.*

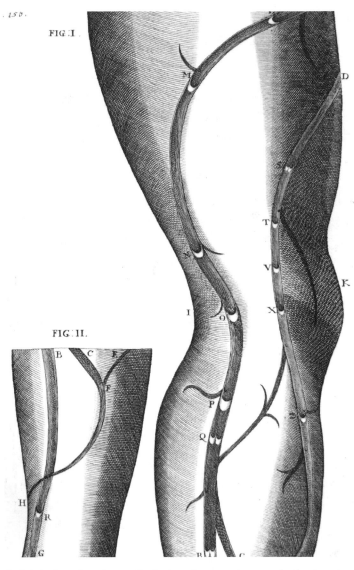

(which is what he called them), opening and closing just enough to regulate the amount of blood flowing *away* from the heart, as Galen had taught. This keeps all the blood from draining downward toward the feet and pooling there. Harvey disagreed with his teacher, pointing out that the "little doors" were found not only in the veins of the arms and legs, but also in those of the neck, where they could not serve this function. By dissecting segments of veins from various animal and human cadavers, Harvey was able to show that a metal probe easily passes through the little doors in the direction of the heart, but cannot be forced through the other way. Harvey showed that these doors swing only one way.

Referring again to the arm with a partially tightened tourniquet, Harvey pointed out that nodes were evident in the swollen veins and that these were in fact the "little doors." For experimental purposes, he recommended that the arm of a lean man who had recently exercised—and therefore was warm and had a good pulse—be used. Then he noted that if one presses down on a swollen vein with one finger, to prevent if from filling from one side, and then uses a finger on the other hand to press the blood out of the space between the first finger and the next node toward the tourniquet, the blood will not return when the second finger is removed, but will do so when the first one is removed. The logical conclusion was that the blood could not flow back through the node, which Harvey called a valve instead of a door, but could readily come from "upstream."

Harvey noted that one can repeat this experiment a thousand times in a brief interval of time, and can thus be "perfectly persuaded" of the circulation of the blood. The reference is to the heart's ability to pump an amount of blood at least as great as what the experimenter presses out of the small segment of swollen vein, and to do so by a thousand beats in less than half an hour. Where could so much blood go in so short a time if it were not driven round in a circuit? He concludes that "reasons" (logical argument) and "ocular" experiments (those done before the eyes of witnesses and which were in principle repeatable) require that circulation be a fact, and that the forceful, systolic contraction of the heart is the only efficient cause of the motion of the blood.

Having established the phenomenon of circulation, Harvey concludes his book with examples of several observations that could be better explained by circulation than by the Galenic physiology, and with some speculations about the heart and its purpose. He thought that the heart probably was the source of the body's vital heat, and that the blood distributed that heat, together with nutriment, to the rest of the body. Thus circulation carries out what the arterial and venous systems were previously thought to accomplish separately. He considered the heart to be a unique cause or instigator in this operation.

Harvey also pointed out that systemic blood circulation also explains certain facts, such as why poison that enters the body at one remote location quickly affects the entire animal and, likewise, why a diseased part can soon lead to general infection and fever. In Harvey's day, certain medicines were often administered externally, even though their effects were considered to be internal. Smashed Cantharides beetles, for example, were applied to the skin in order to increase urination. This method was considered less dangerous than giving Cantharides as an oral medicine, as it was easier to deliver a mild dose by applying it to the skin. Circulation theory made sense of how local application could so quickly affect a distant organ. With these speculations, Harvey moved beyond the purely scientific aspects of his research program to begin exploring practical uses of his theory. By leading future researchers in this direction, Harvey's book completely revolutionized animal physiology and medicine.

Several hundred years before Galen, anatomists in Alexandria had recognized the existence and nature of the heart's valves, but they had not concluded from their knowledge what we now know, that the blood must pass through the lungs, in what we call the pulmonary transit. They believed that the lungs were the point where air or spirit came into the body, but did not imagine that the blood would need to circulate through the lungs in order to transport this spirit to the heart.

Galen also understood the directional nature of the valves and concluded that some blood left the heart and entered the lungs, where it was squeezed out of the "artery-like veins" (pulmonary arteries) into the "vein-like arteries" (pulmonary veins) by the violence of the lungs' contraction during breathing. However, since he did not view the heart as the central organ of the venous system, but regarded the blood as originating in the liver and reaching the heart much as it reached any other part of the body that required and attracted it, he did not conclude that all the blood must circulate through the lungs. That understanding, necessary for Harvey's ideas to make full sense, was reached, first by Ibn an-Nafis in the 13th century, and then in the 16th century by Michael Servetus and Realdo Colombo.

Ibn an-Nafis was an Arab physician who practiced in Cairo. Based on dissection of cadavers, he concluded that the wall (septum) between the right and left sides of the heart was impervious to blood and that the venous blood must therefore pass through the lungs in order to become mixed with air and further refined in the left side of the heart. He was a Muslim writing in Arabic at a time when scholars in the Christian, Latin-speaking world of the western Mediterranean and northern Europe were just beginning to translate Arabic documents, and there is no evidence that his work was known to Western scholars.

THE PULMONARY TRANSIT

Michael Servetus was a medical student at the University of Paris, where he became an anatomical assistant to Johannes Guenter of Andernach. Guenter had revived interest in Galen's anatomical procedure and passed the Galenic tradition on to his student assistants, Andreas Vesalius and Servetus, who practiced vivisection of animals. Servetus's observation that blood flowed to the lungs in a quantity greater than what the lungs needed for nourishment, along with his inability to find any pores or passages through the cardiac septum, led him to believe that the blood must pass through the lungs, where air was added, and then conveyed to the left heart, where it was made into a homogenous mixture of vitalized, arterial blood.

Servetus believed that divine spirit also entered the human body via the lungs and blood and in 1553 he published

An undated manuscript copy of Ibn an-Nafis's 13th-century epitome, a summary of a written work, of Avicenna's Book of the Whole Canon of Medicine, *in which the pulmonary transit of the blood from the heart's right ventricle to the left auricle was described for the first time. At present, no evidence links this early account with 16th-century descriptions by Michael Servetus and Realdo Colombo, but such an influence is possible.*

his account of the pulmonary transit in a book called *The Restitution of Christianity.* The religious ideas in Servetus's book were found to be heretical by the Reformed Protestant leader, John Calvin, and Servetus was put to death in Geneva in 1553. Most copies of his book were destroyed at that time, in an effort to contain his heresy. It is therefore doubtful whether his work was widely known by anatomists. It was certainly not as influential as that of a contemporary, Matteo Realdo Colombo.

Colombo was an anatomist at Padua, where he may have learned Vesalius's technique for opening the chest of a living animal without collapsing the lungs. He published the results of his medical research in *On Anatomy* in 1559. Harvey cites this book, as supporting evidence for the pulmonary transit. Unlike Ibn an-Nafis and Servetus, who had made their arguments on the basis of the much larger than needed supply of venous blood to the lungs, Colombo claimed that the presence of "arterial" blood in the pulmonary veins, which led from the lungs to the left side of the heart, could not be explained adequately unless the blood were to pass through the lungs and become mixed with air in the process.

These three discoverers of the pulmonary transit depended on two anatomical facts: the absence of passages through the cardiac septum, and the belief that the valves of the heart were fluid-tight and permitted only one direction of blood flow: from the right heart to the lungs and the lungs to the left heart. But whereas Ibn an-Nafis had argued on the basis of dissection of cadavers, Servetus and Colombo presented evidence obtained by examining animals, a procedure encouraged by the renewed interest humanist physicians took in Galen's anatomical procedures.

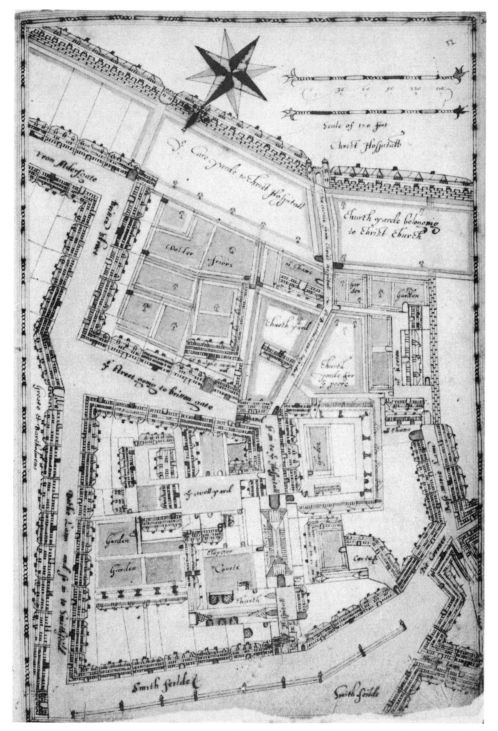

This 1617 plan shows the layout of St. Bartholomew's Hospital in London, when Harvey was a physician. The plan is oriented with north to the lower left corner. Like many medieval hospitals, St. Bartholomew's originated as a monastic foundation. It was located just outside the city wall (at the top), which formed one boundary of the monastery.

Royal Physician and Scholar

For two decades after the 1628 publication of *Anatomical Exercise on the Motion of the Heart and Blood in Animals,* Harvey's life was largely occupied with his service to the Crown. Harvey retained his position at St. Bartholomew's Hospital and remained busy with the College of Physicians, but he was increasingly called upon to attend the king, who often resided away from London. This meant that he had difficulty fulfilling his obligations at St. Bartholomew's, so in 1633 to compensate for his frequent absences, he hired a second physician and reorganized the hospital staff. The apothecary acquired an assistant, and the surgeons were further subordinated to the physicians. The result was a much more vertical structure, with Harvey at the top.

King James died in the spring of 1625, leaving his son Charles I to succeed him. Charles had married Henrietta Marie, the Catholic sister of the French King Louis XIII. For his entire reign as King of England, James had managed to maintain a balance between the restive Puritans and the

Catholic minority in England. Under the new reign of Charles I, the prospect of a new Catholic queen was a threat to this tenuous calm.

The King depended on Parliament for support of the army and maintenance of the fleet. By this time Parliament had come to be predominantly Protestant and represented largely London-based and increasingly wealthy middle-class urban merchants, manufacturers, and captains of industry. The interests of these businessmen were often at odds with the Crown's, both in religion and England's involvement in foreign affairs. The king aimed to retain aristocratic privilege and at the same time lighten the tax burden on the mostly rural, mostly Catholic poor. They were suffering under the new economic order, which shifted the center of production and wealth away from rural agricultural towns to urban trade and heavily capitalized mining and manufacturing ventures.

As Parliament relentlessly maneuvered to limit the royal budget and hamper the Crown's military campaigns, King Charles was forced to seek more and more help from the English Catholics. He grew more alienated from the Protestant majority in both England and Scotland. When he summoned Parliament in 1628, it demanded the right to enforce religious conformity to Calvinism on all of England. Charles I refused, and Parliament adjourned. For the next 11 years, Charles ruled as an absolute monarch, without requiring the consent of Parliament, while the Puritans chafed—or emigrated to the American colonies.

During those difficult years of political and religious tension in England, Harvey grew closer to King Charles, who was an avid collector of art and supporter of the sciences. Toward the end of 1629 the king ordered Harvey to travel abroad in Europe with the Earl of Lennox. To do so, Harvey gave up his second term as treasurer of the College of Physicians and took a leave of absence from St. Bartholomew's Hospital. During his travels in Europe, Charles appointed him Ordinary Physician, with a salary of £300—quite a raise. The new

position meant that Harvey would be fully engaged as the king's personal physician rather than being an occasional consultant. Upon his return to England he would have to be available whenever his services were required.

In October 1633 Harvey accompanied the king to Scotland and then back to London. Two years later he developed a close friendship with the Earl of Arundel, and the king sent the two men on a diplomatic mission to the imperial court at Vienna in 1636. From there, Harvey was sent to Venice, Florence, and Rome, Italy, to procure paintings for the king's private collection. At that time, physicians were often also aesthetics who had traveled and knew art.

During his travels Harvey seems never to have missed an opportunity to examine nature and discuss his ideas with

King Charles I succeeded his father James I as the second Stuart King of England and Scotland. His efforts to govern England autocratically were stymied by Parliament and led to the English Civil War and his own death.

scholars he encountered. On his journey into northern Italy with the Earl of Lennox in 1631, for example, Harvey wrote back to England that the Mantuan Wars, in which France and the Holy Roman Empire fought over control of the frontier principality of Mantua in northern Italy, had so devastated the countryside that scarcely any animals were available to dissect. And while in Germany with the Earl of Arundel, Harvey took the opportunity to visit the renowned physician and teacher Caspar Hofmann. Harvey attempted to convince Hofmann of his theory of circulation by personally demonstrating the ligation of the vessels to prove the direction of blood flow, along with other anatomical experiments described in his 1628 book, but Hofmann remained unpersuaded.

In England, King Charles admired Harvey's skill as an anatomist and gave him ample opportunity to pursue anatomical research, and often brought him deer from the royal hunt to dissect. By examining these deer, which were killed at various ages and at different times of the year, Harvey became familiar with their various stages of reproduction and development. The dissections also served as

William Harvey explains a medical point to King Charles I.

entertainment for the king, who like many European monarchs, took interest in natural philosophy. When the king's senior physician died in 1639, Harvey was promoted to the position, which entitled him to free lodging and meals at Whitehall Palace in London and a salary of £400—a tidy sum. Now housed with the royal family, Harvey also had opportunities to converse with Queen Henrietta's family physician Jean Riolan. Riolan was among the foremost medical teachers and physicians in France. Harvey later directed his only published response to criticisms of his circulation theory to Jean Riolan.

The difficult relations between King Charles and Parliament came to a head in the early 1640s. At this time, not only were the English Protestants causing the king trouble but so were his Scottish subjects, who wished Scotland to be a Protestant nation. They prevailed, and King Charles effectively lost control of "his" Scottish military. Faced with the continuing threat of the Scottish army entering England and siding with the Puritans, the King summoned Parliament with the hope of securing funds to mount an English military defense of one of his kingdoms against the Scottish. However, Parliament feared that the king would use the English army against them, and denied him the money. Instead, Parliament seized control of the government and the army, and the king fled London in January 1642. In desperation, Charles traveled to Nottingham that same year, hoping to raise his own army of Royalists in northern England to retake London. It resulted in the English Civil War between those who supported the Parliament and the Crown on August, 1642.

As a member of the royal court and a loyal follower of the king, Harvey found himself in a difficult situation. His job at St. Bartholomew's Hospital required his presence in London, at least some of the time, but London was firmly under Parliament's control. The College of Physicians, which was composed of many loyalists to the king, was also a London institution and it suffered under the ensuing persecution of Royalist sympathizers.

Heavily taxed by the city authorities, the College was saved from bankruptcy only by the intervention of one of its members, who privately purchased the meeting house and botanical garden on behalf of the College. Harvey's own Royalist sympathies and his position as the senior royal physician demanded that he attend the king, which he did. In defiance of an order of Parliament, Harvey left London to join the king at Nottingham. He was charged with the care of the young princes at Edgehill, where the first large battle of the Civil War was fought. As a result of his choice, St. Bartholomew's stopped payment of his salary the following year. By that time Harvey was with the king at his headquarters in Oxford, and Parliament ordered St. Bartholomew's to replace him.

Harvey took the opportunity of his four-year stay in Oxford to become better acquainted with the university community. In 1645 he was appointed Warden (resident dean) of Merton College. Although these were grim years for the monarchy and for England in general, they must have been somewhat liberating for Harvey. Although he was deprived of his routine duties in London, he was freed to teach and pursue personal research when he was not required to attend the king. He made many close friends and engaged in research and academic conversation with them.

Harvey struck up lifelong friendships with fellow physicians George Bathurst and Charles Scarburgh. With them he undertook close observation of the development of fertilized chicken eggs and studied animal growth and reproduction, a research program that Fabricius had also followed. With Christopher Wren, an Oxford medical student who later became England's premier architect, he studied the anatomy of muscles.

Perhaps it was during these years that Harvey put the finishing touches on his treatise *On the Generation of Animals,*

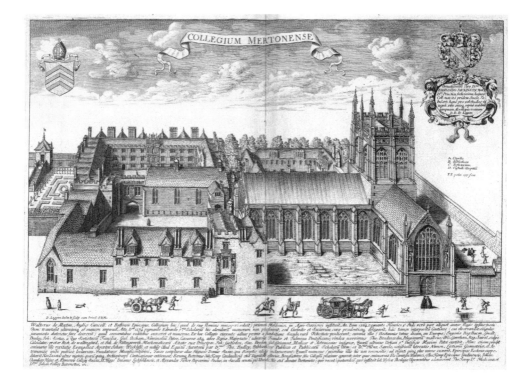

which was circulating as a manuscript at that time. He probably also continued his research on insects and human biology, paying particular attention to clinical observation. Although he had left behind his manuscripts in London at his residence in Whitehall Palace, he undoubtedly expected to finish the books on these subjects. In several respects, these must have been very productive years. Although he was in frequent attendance on the king, he was not traveling so much. Whereas previously he had mostly worked alone, he was enjoying collaboration with some of England's most brilliant scientists and gaining their respect.

In 1646 the Royalist forces were finally defeated, and King Charles fled northward in disguise and surrendered to the Scottish army. Still being their king, he may have hoped to be saved from the English Parliamentarians. Oxford surrendered to the Parliamentary army. Harvey was out of a job. Rather than accompany Charles Scarburgh and the remnant

William Harvey was Warden of Merton College at Oxford University in 1645–46. Harvey's workroom was on the right side, behind the chapel. Oxford was the site of important anatomical and physiological experiments during the 1640s and 1650s because of Harvey's innovations and reputation.

of Royalist forces to Scotland, he chose to go back to London and live at the nearby estate of one of his brothers.

He again became an active member of the College of Physicians. Later that year he persuaded Scarburgh to join him and secured a teaching position for him with the Company of Barber–Surgeons and helped him become a member of the Royal College of Physicians. Meanwhile, the Scottish army sold King Charles to the English Parliamentarians. A little more than a year later, the English

King Charles I receives the last rites on the scaffold before his execution. The turbulent interregnum that followed lasted until 1660.

army seized control of Parliament and ordered it to try King Charles for treason. The king was executed in January 1649, and William Harvey's career as royal physician came to a decisive end.

The execution of the king brought about a political crisis, during which the army ruled by what amounted to military dictatorship, under the control of the Puritan leader Oliver Cromwell, who had risen to prominence during the Civil War. In the years immediately following the king's death, Royalist supporters who remained in England suffered political repression, and sometimes were charged retributive fines aimed at weakening or ruining them financially. Harvey was fined the extraordinary sum of £2,000—the equivalent of five years of his royal salary—which he nevertheless managed to pay.

He had grown to be a wealthy man over the years, for he had possessed several sources of income and few expenses. His lodgings had been provided at the Crown's expense for several years, and he had no children. His wife was dead (when she died is unknown), and rather than maintain his own household he lived with his relatives.

With his enforced leisure, Harvey returned to his Lumley lectureship at the Royal College of Physicians and continued the private biological investigations that had engrossed him for much of his adult life. Perhaps he also still practiced medicine from time to time, although his own health was beginning to decline. It was during this period of his life that his direct influence over the study of anatomy and physiology was reaching its height, based on his work on circulation and his studies of reproduction, embryology, and childbirth. The latter studies were neither as revolutionary nor as important as his discovery of circulation, but they represent a large part of his life's work as a physician and research biologist. They show that these were issues that he and his contemporaries found just as pressing as the nature of the heart and vascular system.

Reproduction was of interest to natural philosophers for several reasons. Aristotle and Galen, the chief ancient authorities on biology and medicine, differed over the role of male and female in sexual reproduction and the developmental sequence of the animal and human embryo. From the Middle Ages to Harvey's day, scholars debated whether to accept Galen's version, in which male and female each contribute seed, and the embryo grows by a process of nutrition, starting with a primitive liver-like organ, or Aristotle's idea that the form of the child is provided by the male, and the embryo grows by virtue of its innate heat, which resides in its primitive heart.

For Aristotle, the female provides merely a place for the embryo to grow, an external source of heat and passive matter to supply nutrition. More generally, debates over the nature of generation, especially the possibility of the spontaneous generation of living entities from dead carcasses and manure piles, continued. Some scholars even ventured the opinion that under the right conditions, man-like creatures called *homunculi* might be grown in a laboratory vessel, an idea that was viewed by all the major organized religions as an abomination and heresy.

Prior to his retirement from royal service, Harvey's busy life as a lecturer, anatomical demonstrator, practicing physician, and active member of the Royal College of Physicians had left him little time for focused scholarly writing. It had, however, afforded him ample opportunity to dissect, record his experiences with patients, and reflect on animal physiology in the course of his work. He probably began writing *Anatomical Exercise on the Motion of the Heart and Blood in Animals* during the 1620s as a result of conclusions that he reached while preparing and presenting the Lumley lectures and pushed it to completion once the idea of circulation occurred to him, in a relatively short time. During the time he was keeping records of his many dissections and other investigations, he also slowly began to compose manuscripts

Gulielmus Harveu
de
Generatione Animalium.

William Harvey's On the Generation of Animals, *was published in 1651 at the urging of his friend George Ent. The frontispiece shows a crowned man opening an egg, which bears the inscription* ex ovo omnia *("all things from an egg"), and various kinds of animals are coming out of it. This emblematic device summarizes Harvey's belief that there is an egg for every form of animal, including insects, which were long thought to arise spontaneously from rotting matter.*

on other subjects, most of which disappeared from his residence at Whitehall Palace when it was ransacked by Puritan parliamentarians in 1642.

Harvey started drafting studies on the reproduction and development of animals during the 1630s; he loaned these to a medical colleague named George Ent, which is probably why they were not destroyed when the royal palace was looted by supporters of Parliament during the Civil War. At Ent's urging, he eventually published the studies as a group under the general title *On the Generation of Animals* in 1651, along with a short tract on the anatomy of the uterus, placenta, and umbilical cord and another on childbirth. Another treatise on muscles and how they produce motion in animals also survived but was not published in Harvey's lifetime.

Lost to the palace looters were a treatise on insects, a study of human pathology, diseases that he planned to publish someday, and—perhaps the greatest loss—his casebooks. These contained the many notes on human anatomy and diseases that he had gleaned from a long career as a physician and anatomist. They were the raw material for his work on morbid anatomy, that is, an attempt to correlate diseases that are diagnosed in living bodies with abnormal anatomical features that are evident after death. Had he carried through his planned study, he would also have contributed much to pathology, the study of how diseases affect the body.

The requirement that medical students witness anatomical demonstrations, which encouraged anatomical research in the late Middle Ages, was important for the knowledge of the body, but it had little immediate effect on medical pathology. This was partly because of the philosophical orientation of the anatomists and partly because of the specimens available. As long as anatomical investigation aimed to establish the "essential form" of the body and its parts—the idealized, defining structures—irregularities in dissected specimens were of minor consequence. The object was to understand what a spleen or a kidney looked like in general—what characteristics made it a spleen or a kidney rather than something else—and not what any particular spleen or kidney might look like, whether healthy or diseased.

This is not to say that medieval physicians were unaware or uninterested in pathology, merely that it was not a goal of systematic anatomical study. Already in 13th-century Italy, physicians performed autopsies in order to determine if prominent persons had been poisoned or had died of natural causes. Certain poisons caused discoloration and enlargement of specific organs, and proper identification assumed that the physician knew what the normal conditions of those organs were. However, in general physicians did not attempt to trace particular anatomical changes to particular conditions of the disease, nor did they demonstrate morbid pathology at the annual university anatomies.

The nature of the bodies that were available for public use and therefore for anatomical research was another reason why anatomical study did not lead to a new pathology. Generally these were men (only occasionally women) who had been convicted of a capital offense and hanged by the authorities. Hanging was the preferred means of execution for ordinary citizens, beheading being reserved for the privileged class. Harvey made several passing references in his works to anatomical effects that he attributed to this manner of death.

Executions were often scheduled to provide fresh material for the annual dissections or they were delayed until the winter, as cadavers did not keep well and could not be easily preserved before the invention of artificial

This 1565 charter, issued by the government of Queen Elizabeth I, granted the Royal College of Physicians each year the bodies of four criminals, who were executed by hanging, to be used for anatomical demonstrations. Such charters guaranteed that suitable fresh corpses were available to late medieval medical schools at the appropriate season for dissection, since the executions could be scheduled.

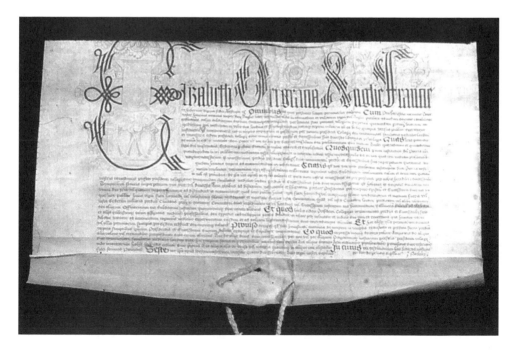

refrigeration. This may seem uncivilized to the modern reader, but during Harvey's time torture and the violent execution of persons convicted of treason and other crimes against the government, followed by public exhibition of their bodies or body parts, was accepted practice. Outside the anatomical demonstrations, human bodies were hard to come by, and the shortage of materials occasionally led to the robbing of fresh graves.

Felix Platter, who studied medicine at the University of Montpellier in southern France a half century earlier in 1554, vividly described how he and his fellow students broke into a cemetery that was looked after by monks from a local monastery. Under the cover of darkness and armed with swords, they stole the freshly-buried cadaver of a deformed woman. On a second visit several days later, they dug up the bodies of a student they had known and a little boy. Distracting the guard who watched the city gate at night, the students sneaked the bodies back to the home of one of their party and dissected them. They boiled the skeleton free of tissue and reassembled and saved it. Alerted to the thefts, the monks vigilantly guarded the cemetery to prevent such grave robbings.

Felix's account points to the dilemma medical students faced in obtaining bodies that they could dissect for themselves and the dire lengths to which they would go to obtain specimens. The event he recorded happened in 1554 but the situation had not changed much by the time Harvey was a student. Dissections depended largely on the cooperation of authorities to provide the bodies of criminals for scheduled public dissections, the desire of the wealthy to determine the cause of death in suspicious cases, and the availability of usually poor people who died in hospitals without relatives to claim their bodies for burial.

The consequence of using the bodies of executed criminals for research was that they were more often male than female, seldom old and never infants or children, and generally not seriously diseased. They were suitable for demonstrating idealized anatomical forms, but this did not further the understanding of problems of childbirth, of abnormalities that occurred in early growth, or of the effects of diseases on particular organs.

However, physicians in cities who worked at hospitals, which served mainly to provide care for the poor, or who could attend private autopsies, were able to gain some knowledge of abnormal anatomy and gynecological problems; their work yielded improved surgical treatises in the 16th and 17th centuries, such as Niccoló of Massa's 1536 *Introduction to Anatomy or the Dissection of the Human Body,* which Harvey consulted. But the main textbooks and teaching demonstrations continued to depict only normal anatomy.

Presentation of normal anatomy through reading and public autopsies also suited another, non-medical purpose—Christian philosophical and religious speculation about what it means to be human and how one might better understand the nature of the Creator (God) by examining the creature that he created in his own image, as the Christian Bible taught. Although Harvey's writings are notably free of such religious speculation, it was a common practice in medical works of the early modern period and well into the 19th century.

Harvey had wide experience with dissection of all kinds, in connection with both his Lumley lectures and presumably also in the course of his work at St. Bartholomew's Hospital. Considering the number of years he lectured and the specific references to results of post-mortem examinations that he made in his published writings, it is reasonable to conclude that he performed at least 40 full dissections of executed criminals and considerably more than 100 autopsies, including those of his father, his sister, and various friends and noblemen associated with the court.

His position as royal physician also afforded opportunities that were not generally available to most physicians. For

Harvey performs an autopsy on Thomas Parr with King Charles I, at far right, looking on. Parr's alleged longevity and health fascinated the king.

example, while he was at court he inspected an unhealed wound in the left side of the eldest son of the Viscount Montgomery. The open wound enabled him to reach in and feel the beating heart, and he noted that its systole coincided with the arterial pulse, just as he had asserted in *Anatomical Exercise on the Motion of the Heart and Blood in Animals.* On another occasion, in 1635, he was summoned by the king to examine Thomas Parr, a man reported to be 152 years old, who had been brought to the royal court as something of an oddity for the amusement of the king. Like many princes and wealthy gentlemen of the 17th century, King Charles was curious about accidents and irregularities of nature. In Parr's case, it is clear that both his longevity and his virility were matters of interest—he was reported to have been sexually active even after his second marriage, at age 122.

Parr had spent several months in London and this had proved too much for the old man and he died. Harvey's account of his post-mortem examination of Parr gives some indication of how he proceeded. He began with a cursory external inspection. Harvey had examined Parr not long before he died and had noted that his face was livid (bluish-red, indicating heart failure) and that he was having difficulty breathing, so he began his internal examination by opening the chest and inspecting the lungs and heart. He found the lungs filled with blood, which was consistent with his diagnosis of pneumonia, and he concluded that Parr had died from the consequent suffocation. When Harvey washed the lungs, however, they had a healthy, milky white appearance. The old man's heart also looked healthy and strong, though with "a considerable quantity of adhering fat."

Harvey next proceeded to the abdomen, noting the general soundness of the intestines, stomach, kidneys, bladder, mesentery, colon, liver, gallbladder, and spleen. With the exception of several small watery abscesses on one kidney and a somewhat undersized spleen, Harvey found nothing unusual, and even remarked that there was no sign of stone in the kidneys or bladder. Stony blockages of the urinary tract were common in early modern Europe, particularly among the upper class, and were sometimes attributed to a wine- and meat-rich diet that the poor generally could not afford. Harvey's assessment of Thomas Parr was as follows: "All the internal parts, in a word, appeared so healthy, that had nothing happened to interfere with the old man's habits of life, he might perhaps have escaped paying the debt due to nature for some little time longer."

Harvey's conclusion that Parr's demise was occasioned by his removal from his simple life to the unhealthy conditions of city and court was more than a physician's admonishment to his noble employer about the effects of luxury; it was classic medical dietary theory, which had its origins in the teachings of Hippocrates in the 5th century BCE. The Hippocratic treatises, written by Hippocrates and his followers and a valued source of medical knowledge in Harvey's day, attributed many illnesses to imbalanced diet and environmental factors.

Harvey had noted that Parr's intestines were strong and healthy, as befitted a man accustomed to eating simple, coarse peasant fare. He figured that Parr's demise was caused by his change in habits after being relocated to London. There he not only ate richer food, but was also exposed to an atmosphere polluted with the stench of decomposing waste and garbage, "to say nothing of the smoke engendered by the general use of sulphurous coal as fuel," Harvey noted. The change from sunny, well-ventilated rural England had been the death of the old man.

Thomas Parr's case was exceptional in that the written account of Harvey's autopsy survived and was eventually published, but there is no reason to suppose that Harvey proceeded much differently in this autopsy than he must have in many others, taking note of an enlarged spleen here and a cancerous liver there. The accumulation of such data was an important first step toward correlating specific diseases with specific pathological changes in the body. But even if Harvey had published his treatise or his casebooks, real breakthroughs in pathology would have to wait until systematic case studies could be evaluated in light of different theories about what diseases are and how they develop, which did not happen in the late 18th and 19th centuries.

Although Harvey's work on pathology did not lead to a book, he finally published his book on animal development in 1651. This was read by a generation of medical scholars who had already confronted his theory of circulation, and those who accepted it were beginning to cope with the collapse of the old Galenic physiology. Amid the proliferation of new studies, Harvey's ideas concerning the development of the embryo were much less novel, although they would have been provocative at the time he actually formulated them early in his career.

There was little serious disagreement in the medieval university about general organic development because Galen and medical writers after him generally confined their scholarship and personal observation to medicine and human biology. But when it came to human reproduction and fetal development, arguments abounded, fueled by many of the same underlying philosophical, religious, and legal issues that affect decisions about medical interventions and abortions today: What is the essence of a developing human? When does the embryo receive its immortal soul (a matter taken for granted in medieval and early modern Europe) and become a human being? In what part of the body does the soul reside?

Harvey, following Aristotle, carefully studied the development of chicken embryos by selecting a large batch of eggs that had been laid on the same day and opening one each day. Harvey floated the contents of each egg in warm water in a glass vessel and discerned the first sign of motion, of life, to be a tiny pulsating spot of red blood, which was visible when it expanded but invisible in contraction. This spot grew to become a small heart-like structure, with a developing network of blood vessels attached. Aristotle had made a similar observation and concluded from it that the heart was the rudiment of the embryo, the primary organ, which preceded all others in development. In Harvey's words, the heart was "the first thing that lives and the last that dies." This was an observation that fit well with the ancient and persistent idea that the heart is the center of human feeling, the center of one's being.

The observation of the tiny "leaping point" of blood, as Harvey called it, and Aristotle's interpretation of it as the rudimentary heart, did not agree with Galen's theories, either about human development or about human physiology. Galen believed that development required nutrition, and that the principle organ of nutrition was the liver. It was the liver that took the semi-digested nutrients and made them into venous blood, which flowed through the veins and supplied both the embryo and the adult with what they needed to grow and thrive. Therefore, the liver or some primitive organ that served its blood-making function must precede the other parts, or else develop simultaneously with them. One can appreciate the logical dilemma that Aristotelian embryology posed for Harvey and others: how could the heart and its blood appear before the liver, if the liver was necessary to make the blood that was sent to the heart? The only way to reconcile Galen's physiology, which required the liver to develop before the heart and other organs, with Aristotle's embryology, which claimed that the heart was the first observed organ, was to assume that the liver really preceded the heart in development, but was invisible.

Harvey, however, did not care to speculate much about the unseen. In an age of religious strife, he spoke little about how biological design might reflect the work of divine intelligence. He was a convinced Aristotelian, but generally avoided discussion of the final causes or purposes of things, which Aristotelians regarded as their ultimate significance. In an era marked by a proliferation of metaphysical theories about the nature of matter, space, and motion, Harvey preferred to write about what he could see, test experimentally, and reasonably deduce from his observations. Accordingly, he rejected the idea that the human body took in any kind of spirit at all, as Galenists believed. He did not believe that spirit was something separable from the human body, something which could be eaten or inhaled and joined with it.

Harvey thought there was only one spirit, one soul, and it was either in the blood before birth or else was the blood itself. His observation was that the "leaping point" visible in the early embryo was not the heart, but blood. The blood, then, was endowed with everything it needed to create the rest of the embryo—first the heart and later the liver and other organs. The lungs, which were late to form and even later to function, because breathing did not commence until birth or hatching, were obviously not instrumental in embryonic physiology. So inspiration of some sort of spirit or vital power from the air was obviously unnecessary to the life of the embryo. In chicken eggs it was fairly obvious that not much respiration could be coming from outside the egg.

Harvey's investigation of pregnant deer, similarly showed no direct connections between the fetal vascular system and that of the mother by which spirit might come to the embryo. All these observations led Harvey, although logical, to what turned out to be the wrong conclusion—that breathing serves only to cool the blood.

Harvey's theories, like all embryology, had important consequences for the understanding of respiration and circulation. If Harvey was right about the blood preceding all else, then Galen was wrong about more than just circulation and the anatomy of the heart. If Harvey was right about the essence of the animal's life, its vitality and soul, being vested in the blood, then how could one justify Galen's therapeutic system, in which blood was but one of four constituent fluids whose balance regulated health? If, as Harvey argued, blood was life, was it possible that the matter of the blood

Harvey noted his own comments by penning a "WH" next to the Lumlean lectures, as shown in this note from about 1617. He kept notes that he reworked as he repeated his Lumley lectures at the Royal College of Physicians. Harvey's own notes serve as a guide to the development of his thinking about the motion of the heart.

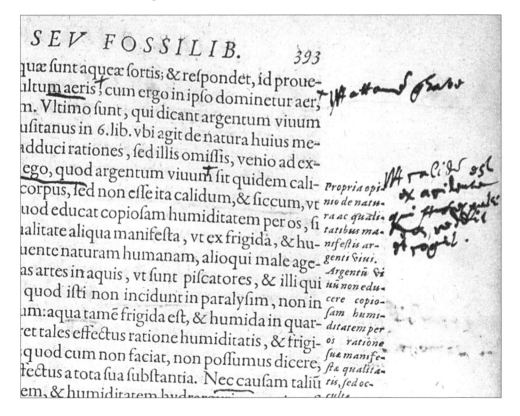

itself was what caused growth? Did matter contain life and give rise to life, as studies on the growth of crystals and spontaneous appearance of flies from manure had led some to believe?

Such ideas serve as foundations of ideologies, and bear on our philosophy of nature as well as on religion, politics, and social order. They did so then and they continue to do so now. For this reason, cultural historians have examined the work of people like Harvey for clues about shifting ideas that pertain to the social, political, and religious thinking of a particular society.

Did Harvey's opinion about the special nature of the blood, which was developed particularly in his book *On the Generation of Animals,* signal a conceptual change from his first publication, where he focused on the heart as the primary organ, the first to live and last to die? Did his later emphasis on the life of the blood, which circulates throughout the "commonwealth" of the body, contrast with his early emphasis on the heart as the king of the body, whose purpose and function was to serve the whole body and not just its own needs? In short, did Harvey's biology reflect his views about the Crown and the governance of England? If so, this was not the first instance, nor the last, in which political and social theory found corroboration and legitimacy in natural philosophy. After all, the orderly flow of power from the king to the peasant and from the Pope to the common Christian was considered to be as natural as the flowing down or "influence" of celestial power onto the subordinate earth.

In Harvey's case, the answer seems to be that Harvey did not shape his conception of the body to project a social or political idea. Examination of Harvey's manuscript lecture notes, which he compiled in 1616 for his first Lumley lectures and then added to it over the next decade or more, reveals that he already believed then blood to be the origin of the embryonic body. He also understood that this finding contradicted both Aristotle, who thought the heart was primary, and Galen, who argued for the primacy of the liver.

As Harvey's specific study of the heart and blood took shape, his belief in the primacy of the blood in no way conflicted with his argument that the heart is the primary *organ* of the body. As his ideas about physiology developed over the years, his commitment to the singular importance of the blood solidified. The blood was the source of vitality. It heated the heart, not the other way around. Debate on this point occupied the minds of those who considered the merits and deficiencies of his book *Anatomical Exercise on the Motion of the Heart and Blood in Animals.*

Harvey did not abandon or seriously change his views on the heart and blood in his mature years and he never abandoned his loyalty to the Crown or belief in monarchy as the proper form of government, even though to do so must have been a tempting, practical choice once the monarch was dead and Parliament ruled the country. Harvey's own experimental method, which he alluded to in his writings, suggests that he preferred to leave speculations about things that were not accessible to the senses undecided; he built his natural philosophy on experiment and observation.

The Reception of Harvey's Ideas

From a modern perspective, Harvey's arguments for the circulation of the blood through the body seem clear-cut and persuasive. His use of experimental evidence combined with lucid reasoning based on his observations is quite convincing. So it is somewhat difficult for us to understand that his discovery was not immediately accepted by all who read his book, or even by those persons fortunate enough to witness his anatomical demonstrations. Perhaps more surprising is the fact that even though some of Europe's best medical minds agreed with Harvey on certain details, such as the action of the heart and arteries, they still failed to grasp what for us is the obvious consequence—the circulation of the blood from the arteries into the veins through the body's various tissues, and from the veins to the arteries by way of the heart and lungs. Other scholars accepted this idea of circulation, but rejected Harvey's theory that the heart impelled the blood through the lungs and the body by contracting forcefully.

The initial reaction to Harvey's discovery was mixed. Some of his contemporaries were reluctant to abandon a theoretical system that had adequately explained clinical observations for centuries. And some were unconvinced

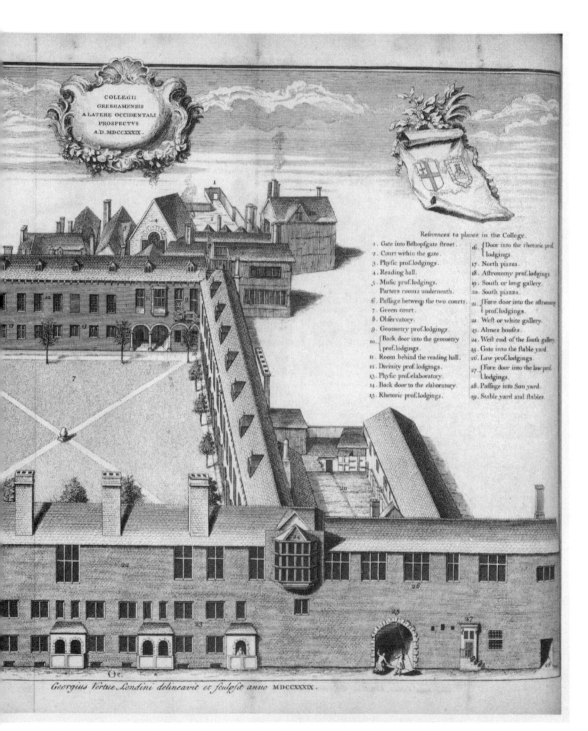

COLLEGII GRESHAMENSIS A LATERE OCCIDENTALI PROSPECTVS A.D. MDCCXXXIX.

References to places in the College.

1. Gate into Bishopfgate ftreet.
2. Court within the gate.
3. Phyfic prof. lodgings.
4. Reading hall.
5. Mufic prof. lodgings. Porters rooms underneath.
6. Paffage between the two courts.
7. Green court.
8. Obfervatory.
9. Geometry prof. lodgings.
10. { Back door into the geometry prof. lodgings.
11. Room behind the reading hall.
12. Divinity prof. lodgings.
13. Phyfic prof. elaboratory.
14. Back door to the elaboratory.
15. Rhetoric prof. lodgings.
16. { Door into the rhetoric prof. lodgings.
17. North piazza.
18. Aftronomy prof. lodgings.
19. South or long gallery.
20. South piazza.
21. { Fore door into the aftronomy prof. lodgings.
22. Weft or white gallery.
23. Almes houfes.
24. Weft end of the fouth gallery.
25. Gate into the ftable yard.
26. Law prof. lodgings.
27. { Fore door into the law prof. lodgings.
28. Paffage into Sun yard.
29. Stable yard and ftables.

Georgius Vertue, Londini delineavit et fculpfit anno MDCCXXXIX.

Many of the important physiological experiments that followed up on Harvey's discovery of the blood circulation were demonstrated at the new Royal Society, which was formally announced in 1660 at Gresham College in London. The Royal Society met at Gresham College and Arundel House until new quarters were found in 1710.

that experimental evidence was relevant to physiological research. Others doubted Harvey's ideas because they lacked proper grounding in metaphysics, the traditional philosophical principles that were used to explain the world.

Many physicians and philosophers were steeped in the classics and convinced of the time-tested scholastic method of arriving at truth by debating the strengths and weaknesses of theories on the basis of authoritative opinions and the logical structure of the arguments that were presented. Such scholars did not readily understand or approve Harvey's methods, which called for firsthand experiment, observation, comparative analysis, and logical reasoning about the relation of structures to their functions. Indeed, acceptance of Harvey's circulation theory turned out to be largely dependent on the age and social standing of the reader. Anatomists and physicians of Harvey's generation, many of whom had a vested interest in maintaining the standard medical curriculum, generally refused to admit that he was correct. On the other hand, their students who were interested in a more hands-on approach often hastened to recreate Harvey's experiments and see for themselves, and then agreed with his conclusions.

Prior to Harvey, new anatomical discoveries had not seriously undermined the traditional physiology that Galen had put together from the writings of the best medical authorities of Greek antiquity and then rigorously shaped into a coherent system on the basis of his own medical practice and scientific education. The universities of Harvey's day required professors to teach a curriculum that was based on Galen's teachings and specified by the universities' statutes. This maintained educational standards but also discouraged innovation.

Harvey's colleagues at the Royal College of Physicians—London's best-educated M.D.s—were therefore understandably skeptical of his account of the functioning of the heart and the circulation of the blood, which ran contrary to what they had been taught. But then, Harvey was not writing for them. Even though he claimed to be publishing his ideas at their urging, his audience was more likely a cadre of his intellectual peers, European anatomists who were interested not just in medicine, but also in human and animal physiology. Harvey's choice to have *Anatomical Exercise on the Motion of the Heart and Blood in Animals* published in Frankfurt, Germany, rather than in London probably reflects not only his anxiety about the reception that English physicians had given his ideas when he presented them in his lectures, but also his desire to make his work more international.

In March of 1630, another member of the Royal College of Physicians, James Primrose, published his reaction to Harvey's theory in a book called *Exercises and Observations on the Book about the Motion of the Heart.* He rejected Harvey's circulation of blood theory outright and attempted to explain all of Harvey's observations on the basis of Galenic theory. For example, he argued that arteries are thicker than veins not because they must withstand the force of the blood's pressure, but because they must contain the vital spirits that Galenists assumed were transported by the arterial system. Such spirits, regarded as materially very thin, would easily penetrate the walls of the arterial vessels, if they were as thin as the walls of the veins and would escape into the body. Primrose also asserted that the heart has a "pulsific virtue" that causes it to beat and rejected the idea that it is a muscle, forcefully contracting in systole. After all, muscles were generally thought to be voluntary instruments, and clearly the heart beat without conscious command.

Throughout his response to Harvey, Primrose appealed to written authority, quoting Galen and Vesalius, rather than presenting any experimental evidence to refute Harvey's claims. He even went so far as to claim that the heart did indeed have small pores in the septum between the right and left ventricles, as Galen had written. He quoted Vesalius as his authority on this point, but he must have been reading the 1543 first edition of the great anatomist's *On the Architecture of the Human Body* because Vesalius had come to deny the existence of such pores by the second edition, published in 1555.

One would think that Primrose's utter rejection and specific attack would have upset Harvey and taken him by surprise. Not many months had passed since Harvey had sat on the examination board that approved Primrose's admission to the Royal College of Physicians in December of 1629, and Primrose's book was published in London, where it was readily available to Harvey's peers. But Harvey did not publish a response to Primrose, perhaps because his duties to the king required him to travel abroad extensively in the 1630s, or perhaps because Primrose was really just raising the same speculative points that Harvey's experimental evidence had already disproved, and there was little to be gained by publishing a reply. It would be up to others to answer Primrose's objections.

Harvey met many medical scholars, students, and physicians during the course of his travels in England and Scotland and in Europe and he must have taken the opportunity to explain and occasionally demonstrate how he believed the cardiovascular system worked. Certainly his journeys abroad in the early- and mid-1630s coincided with academic debate about circulation of the blood, as numerous letters and published responses to his book attest. In 1630, for instance, the great Danish professor of medicine, royal physician, and collector of natural objects and artifacts, Ole Worm, wrote to a Danish medical student named Jacob Svabe at Leiden University, inquiring what reception Harvey's ideas had received there. By this time Leiden University was beginning to replace University of Padua as the leading university for medical education, so the reaction there to Harvey's ideas was very important for acceptance in the rest of Europe.

Svabe replied to Worm that he was very excited about Harvey's discoveries, as was his fellow student Hermann

Conring. Their professors, though, were understandably cautious about giving up the old theory without clear anatomical evidence that the blood flows through the body, and Ole Worm agreed. Worm did not accept the possibility that blood could leave the smallest arteries, infiltrate small pores in the tissues, and reenter the smallest veins, because experience showed that blood quickly coagulated once it left the blood vessels. He was also skeptical of the idea that there were small interconnections between the veins and arteries in the lungs, on the grounds that blood contained in the veins was too thick to pass into the smallest arteries. Like many of his generation, he was unable to cast aside centuries-old wisdom in favor of Harvey's experiments and interpretations.

Hermann Conring had initially been skeptical of Harvey's claims. But beginning in 1632 he was defending them at Helmstadt, Germany, where he taught Aristotelian natural philosophy and undertook his own research. In his treatise *On the Generation and Natural Motion of the Blood,* finished in 1643 and published three years later at Leiden University, he recounted how Harvey's argument that the valves of the veins enforce movement of the blood toward the heart had encouraged him to investigate circulation for himself; his own experiments on live animals convinced him that Harvey was correct.

Harvey's ideas also soon won over the leading anatomical teachers at Rotterdam, Zacharias Sylvius and Jacobus de Back, who began to teach circulation in 1633. By the end of the decade, circulation theory was generally accepted there and at Leiden University, where Harvey's experiments were being repeated and even extended by Franciscus Sylvius, who began lecturing about and demonstrating Harvey's account of the motion of the heart and blood in 1638. Sylvius' student Johannes Walaeus' experimental work proved very influential in convincing European medical students of the validity of Harvey's results. Walaeus had earlier been introduced to the circulation theory by Johann

Vesling, who had met Harvey in 1636 and later corresponded with him.

Walaeus's careful reconstructions of Harvey's demonstrations convinced many, and several of his new experiments also proved to be useful to Harvey himself, who tacitly adopted them several years later. Walaeus opened up the leg of a living dog and exposed the main artery and vein. He ligated, or tied off, the vein and noted that the portion nearer the heart emptied of blood, whereas the part toward the foot swelled up with blood and became quite tight, as did the corresponding artery. When the ligature was removed, blood immediately flowed toward the heart in the vein, relieving the swollen vessels. When he ligated the artery, the side toward the heart became engorged with blood, while the side toward the foot emptied and collapsed. With the artery still ligated, he also tied off the vein, which now did not cause swelling, indicating that blood was not entering the vein from the foot side. This experiment was in principle similar to Harvey's earlier tourniquet experiment on the human arm, but was more precise, as Walaeus was able to independently block the flow of the artery and vein and see the effects directly.

Modifying his experimental setup, Walaeus propped up the exposed artery and vein and tied a tight tourniquet around the dog's leg beneath them, excluding the possibility that any blood could come into the limb without passing through one of the two vessels. Then he tied off the vein and severed it on the foot side, and the blood flowed out freely. When he then tied the vein shut further toward the foot, the blood flow ceased, proving that the blood came from the extremity. The only possible supply to the foot was the unligated artery, proving Harvey's claim that the blood enters the extremities via the arteries and returns via the veins.

It would be tempting to believe that when skeptics performed Harvey's experiments or saw them competently demonstrated, they would immediately accept Harvey's

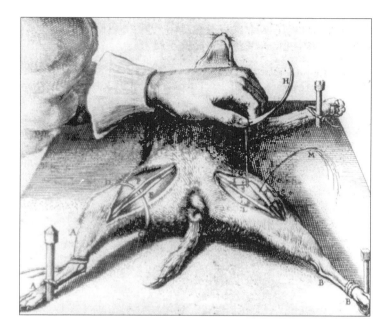

Johannes Walaeus demonstrated Harvey's theory that the blood circulates from the arteries to the veins by selectively tying off (ligating) and opening the crural artery and its paired vein in the leg of a living dog. Such experiments verified Harvey's theory, sometimes with techniques that improved on Harvey's demonstrations. By this choice of experiment, Walaeus showed that blood returning from the end of the leg, through the vein, can only originate from its paired artery, proving that the blood must pass from the artery to the vein.

ideas of circulation of the blood through the lungs and the general circulation of the blood through the body tissues and the operation of the heart. His book is so compelling today because we can readily imagine his procedures and follow his deductive reasoning from one step to another, nodding at each revelation. But such was not the case in the decades after his book left the press. The response of Caspar Hofmann, one of Europe's premier professors of medicine in those years, indicates that Harvey's reasoning and supporting evidence counted for little when one could not agree on the proper questions to ask and the appropriate methods for framing and supporting answers to them.

Harvey and Hofmann met at the University of Altdorf, which Harvey visited while traveling in Germany with the Earl of Arundel on the king's business. For several days in May of 1636, Harvey performed anatomical demonstrations of the motion of the blood before Hofmann, who had also been trained at the University of Padua by the great Fabricius. But as a subsequent exchange of letters reveals, Harvey left Altdorf without convincing his colleague.

Harvey met Caspar Hofmann at Altdorf, Germany, in 1636 and personally showed him some of his anatomical evidence for the circulation of the blood. Hofmann remained unconvinced.

Hofmann accepted pulmonary circulation as necessary for the proper cooling of the blood and nourishment of the lungs, but denied that the heart was simply a muscle. He also rejected the idea that blood circulates from the arteries to the veins. Hofmann's criticism of Harvey's argument for circulation zeroed in on two key weaknesses, one obvious from a modern experimental perspective, and the other very revealing of the influence of contemporary philosophical ideas on the interpretation of new theories.

First, Hofmann agreed with Harvey that blood did not pass through invisible pores in the thick septum that separates the ventricles, from the venous side to the arterial side. He agreed that since no pores were visible, the movement of the blood through the lungs was a better explanation than assuming that undetectable pores existed. But by a similar reasoning, Hofmann asserted, why should he accept Harvey's claim that blood moved from the smallest arteries to the smallest veins, when no passages or connections were visible there?

Second, Hofmann pointed out that Harvey had failed to demonstrate *why* the blood circulated. If the purpose of the blood was to nourish the body and provide it with invisible vital spirits that were thought to account for the difference between the living and the dead, then it would be not only unnecessary but inefficient to send the blood out to the extremities and then call it back before it was used up. The

Galenists' assumption that the parts of the body attract blood nutrients as they needed them was a much more sensible explanation and did not require invisible and therefore unverifiable passages. Here Hofmann agreed with Primrose: the idea that nature was well designed and efficient dictated that the "attractive" faculty in the body's parts would not attract more blood than was required for nutrition. Also, there was no "retro" faculty to explain the attraction of the blood back to the heart through the veins.

The second argument, that Harvey had not shown that circulation served any necessary purpose, was by early 17th-century standards a much more telling criticism of Harvey's account than was the absence of visible connections between arteries and veins. Seventeenth-century scientific theories were full of assumed, hypothetical causes, invisible connections known as sympathies and harmonies, and unexplained tendencies that accounted for why things behaved as they did, so the postulation of unseen conduits was not a radical proposition. But to have failed to prove that circulation was purposeful was to leave the new theory without philosophical support, without a metaphysical explanation.

According to the philosophy of Aristotle, in which both Harvey and Hofmann had been schooled, every natural, physical phenomenon had four "causes" that were necessary to its essence. A phenomenon was composed of a particular combination of material elements (the "material cause"), possessed a characteristic form (the "formal cause"), was created by some kind of process or creative agent (the "efficient cause"), and served a defined purpose (the "final cause"). The "final" referred to the "end" toward which something developed, and the final cause was probably the most important one in Harvey's world. This was not only because purpose was a crucial component of Aristotle's and Galen's ideas about the structure of nature, but also because it was a concept central to the Christian world view.

For Aristotle, "nature abhors a vacuum" and takes measures to prevent empty spaces; this principle explained such phenomena as water rising in a straw when one sucks on it. Any early modern Christian understood that an organ such as the hand or eye had a particular form and composition because it conformed to the divine plan, which built it for a particular purpose. This is called "the argument from design" and is still invoked by fundamentalist Christian critics of Darwinian biology and geology. It was also a key Aristotelian argument against Harvey, inasmuch as Harvey's theory did not explain a purpose for circulation.

Caspar Hofmann's concern for the formal, philosophical integrity of theory also caused him to discount Harvey's experimental evidence, some of which he must have witnessed firsthand at Altdorf, Germany. He found Harvey's quantitative argument impressive, but unsubstantiated and not properly philosophical—again, a reaction that was grounded in 17th-century sensibility. Although today we recognize Harvey's reasoning about the amount of blood that must be leaving the heart and entering the arteries every half hour, and even praise it as a harbinger of modern quantitative methods, Hofmann followed Aristotle and subordinated mathematics to causal reasoning. A quantitative argument was "arithmetic" and was no substitute for proper philosophical (causal) explanation. Besides, as Primrose had contended, Harvey had not proved that any more than a few drops of blood actually left the heart at each beat.

From the modern point of view, the problem with Hofmann's position is that he was permitting the explanation of the facts to determine the establishment of the facts. Harvey also recognized this. In his reply to Hofmann, Harvey pointed out that in chapters eight and nine of his book he had deliberately avoided speaking about final causes and had added no philosophical speculation about nature's reasons for circulation to his summary in the fourteenth chapter. He had confidence in his experimental evidence and was content at that point to discover how the body works. Discussion of causes and purposes should come after the establishment of the facts and not determine the facts: "Because the purpose of the circulation is unknown it does not follow that the phenomenon does not exist," he observed.

He had demonstrated at the dissection table that blood was pushed away from the heart in the arteries at a rate greater than the body could require for nutrition, and he had shown that the blood returned to the heart in the veins. The valves in the veins ensured that. This evidence logically required the transfer of blood from the arteries to the veins through the tissues. He had established that circulation must take place, but he did not wish to speculate why.

Harvey never published a formal refutation of Hofmann's objections. Indeed, what could he do but restate his evidence, perhaps adding an experiment or two, and re-derive the same conclusions that he had reached in 1628. Hofmann for his part never accepted the entire circulation theory. One of his students, Paul Slegel, quickly concluded that Harvey was right, and in 1638 attempted in vain to persuade Hofmann. However, he eventually realized that his mentor had too much of his own academic career invested in Galenic physiology to abandon it completely. Years later, in 1650, Slegel likened the slow acceptance of circulation to the reluctance of the common person to accept Copernicus's idea that the sun was at the center of the universe.

The role of the heart in the circulation of the blood was further confused by the French philosopher René Descartes. Descartes is best known for having introduced the idea that all things in nature, apart from humans minds, function mechanically, without autonomous internal activities or intelligence. This approach to nature is called mechanical philosophy. By 1632 he had read Harvey's book and discussed it with certain correspondents, but did not publish his reaction until 1637, when he described circulation as a

René Descartes agreed with William Harvey's idea that the blood circulated in the human body, but he rejected Harvey's experimental study of how the heart actually moves and functions as a muscular pump. Descartes sought a theory of the heart that was based on entirely mechanical principles, that the heart heats the blood until it vaporizes, which then inflates the heart and pressurizes the arteries.

mechanical, hydraulic process in his widely read *Discourse on Method.*

Although he accepted the concept of circulation, Descartes differed from Harvey when it came to the nature and operation of the heart. Harvey understood the heart to be muscular and to expel the blood into the arteries by means of a forceful, systolic contraction. Descartes envisioned it as a passive vessel that heats the blood to the point of vaporization; the vaporized blood then inflates the heart and pressurizes the arteries, causing the pulse that is evident to the touch. The blood gradually cools and condenses in the extremities, then returns to the heart through the veins to be heated and vaporized anew. Descartes's view of circulation as an evaporation cycle was a kind of hybrid between Harvey's circulation and the views of Aristotle and the followers of Paracelsus who described nature's processes in terms of boiling, fermentation, distillation, and other chemical reactions.

Descartes's ideas (referred to as "Cartesian") were enthusiastically debated in Europe. Both the traditional Aristotelian philosophy and the newer views of the chemists assumed that matter had hidden qualities and capacities, called "faculties," or else active spirits that accounted for observable changes in things. Galenic medicine explained nutrition, growth, excretions, and all other aspects of human physiology in terms of "faculties" of attraction, retention, and expulsion, all of which explained organic functions. Therefore, Harvey's explanation that the heart beats because it has a "pulsific virtue," that it is its natural function to contract and expel blood, did not strike traditional physicians as circular reasoning.

However, students of natural philosophy in the 1640s and 1650s were particularly taken with the idea that changes in the natural world could be explained by a handful of simple physical principles, such as those offered by Descartes and Harvey. The older generation was less enthusiastic, especially those who were familiar with organic development, which seemed to be self-organizing and governed by an internal plan or divine intelligence. University theologians and church authorities generally opposed Descartes's views on religious grounds, as there was little need for an active presence of God in Descartes's universe.

Descartes's adoption of the concept of circulation, which was associated with Harvey in the minds of his contemporaries, often resulted in Harvey's claims being implicated in the debates over Cartesian mechanism, even though Harvey's account was quite different from the Cartesian view of the heart as a machine.

During the first two decades after the publication of his ground-breaking work Harvey did not venture to defend it against the criticisms of James Primrose and Caspar Hofmann or against the modifications made by Descartes and his followers, whose mechanical philosophy Harvey must have wholly rejected as a convinced Aristotelian. These were years of personal and professional turmoil for Harvey. They were marked by frequent travel and by the Civil War that engulfed the royal family and its supporters. After the king's execution in 1649, Harvey was free to return to writing and publication. He then undertook to answer his most recent critic, Jean Riolan.

Harvey and Riolan probably met in the late 1630s, when Riolan came to England as personal physician to Maria de' Medici, the mother of Queen Henrietta Marie of England, the wife of Charles I. Harvey and Riolan became personally acquainted, as well as being professional colleagues. Riolan was also a professor of medicine at the University of Paris, which predisposed him to defend Galenic anatomy and physiology. The Paris medical faculty had been a center of the revival of Galenic anatomy in the 16th century, under the guidance of Vesalius's teacher, Guinter of Andernach. It had become staunchly committed to defending traditional medicine. And Parisian physicians in general were conservative and most of them rejected Harvey's circulation as one more baseless novelty.

When Riolan first learned of Harvey's ideas, he dismissed them as not useful to medical practice. He accepted the experiments showing that the valves in the veins forced at least some of the blood to flow toward the heart but he did not believe in the pulmonary transit or the greater circulation of the blood. He eventually published his formal rejection of circulation of blood in two treatises, the first of which appeared in 1648 and the second the following year.

Unlike Harvey, who had studied both Aristotelian biology and Galenic medicine at University of Padua, Riolan was a Galenic doctor through and through. He was not prepared to accept the goals, procedures, or conclusions of Harvey's "Aristotelian" research program, which treated humans and animals alike as biological entities that were subject to the same physiological laws. Like Primrose, Riolan ridiculed Harvey's investigation of reptiles and fish as childish and not relevant to the physiology of humans. As a Galenist, Riolan was primarily concerned with the integrity of the medical profession as a healing endeavor, and the threat that Harvey's claims posed for therapeutics, the actual diagnosis and treatment of diseases, is probably what motivated him to respond.

Riolan argued that Harvey's circulation theory would destroy the foundations of Galenic physiology and with it the entire therapeutic system. This system depended on relieving *plethora,* or excesses of fluids, chiefly by purging patients by giving them drugs that caused them to vomit, urinate, sweat, or defecate and—in the case of fevers, inflammations, and swellings—by bleeding them.

By the 17th century, the rationale behind bleeding had been elaborated considerably; Galenic physicians believed that letting blood from an inflamed part of the body would relieve the inflammation. An alternate method called for diverting the blood from accumulating in (and corrupting) the afflicted part by letting blood from another, distant part of the body. For instance, a pain in the right side of the chest might lead the physician to bleed from

the patient's right arm. But how could such a theory, backed by centuries of explanation and clinical experience, hold true if the blood was in fact constantly circulating? Those who agreed with Harvey accepted the idea that the blood was systemic, not localized, so bleeding from one location would merely reduce the blood supply throughout the body.

Although bleeding as a therapeutic measure did not end with the acceptance of circulation—it became more excessive in early-19th-century American practice—Riolan was quite acute in observing that Harvey's ideas would require that the foundations of medical theory be rebuilt. His solution was to adopt a compromise. He credited Harvey, Walaeus, and others with performing insightful experiments on living creatures. He even admitted that blood might sometimes be seen

This engraving shows Jean Riolan, a French royal physician and professor of anatomy and pharmacy, in 1626, a decade before he and William Harvey met in England. Riolan's rejection of Harvey's account of circulation prompted Harvey to publish his Two Exercises on the Circulation of the Blood in 1649 in defense of his argument.

text continues on page 116

GALEN'S ARTERIAL TUBE EXPERIMENT

For modern scientists experiments are the arbiters of the truth of hypotheses. An experiment chosen specifically to verify or falsify a hypothesis is called a "crucial experiment." Historians associate experimentation with the rise of modern science in the 17th century, when the crucial experiment was employed in just this way.

Of course, the success of an experiment depends not just on its design, but also on the complexity of the phenomenon being examined and on how the results are interpreted. A crucial experiment can fail to give satisfactory results until the procedures can be adequately refined. A particularly interesting example is the experiment designed by Galen of Pergamon in the second century CE and revisited by physiologists in the 16th and 17th centuries.

The hypothesis questioned by Galen had postulated that the pulse evident in human arteries is the result of the arteries being forcibly filled and dilated by the action of the heart. This had been the view of Erasistratus, one of Galen's predecessors, whose expertise in dissection and vivisection set the standard for Galen's own research. Erasistratus taught that the heart filled the arteries with *pneuma,* a kind of spirit or air that was thought to be inhaled, enlivening the body and causing the regular, living pulse.

Galen rejected Erastistratus's idea that the arteries are usually filled with air, offering several experiments to demonstrate that they are normally filled with blood. If so, what could explain the pulse? Galen's solution was to argue that the pulse was not caused by the blood, but by the arteries, which possessed a "faculty" of expansion.

According to Galen, the arterial pulse was an impulse sent out from the heart through the arterial walls. To disprove Erasistratus's theory and confirm his own, Galen performed an experiment that had many of the characteristics of what came to be called a crucial experiment: If the pulsation of an artery was caused by the pulsation of the flow of air or blood, then it should not be interrupted by the insertion into the blood vessel of an open-ended hollow tube, which was then tightly secured by a ligature, or noose, around the artery holding the tube. If, however, the pulsation was an impulse that was propagated along the arterial wall, then it should be interrupted by the tight ligature. The conception was brilliant.

Galen recorded this experiment in a treatise called "Whether the Blood is Naturally Contained in the Arteries," and again described it in the seventh book of *On Anatomical Procedures,* probably the most important text in the revival of medical anatomy in the 16th century. When he conducted this experiment on a large artery in the leg near the groin (probably the femoral artery in a dog or a pig), he observed that the side of the artery nearer the heart from the ligature continued to pulse, but the farther side no longer throbbed. Galen concluded that this result had disproved Erasistratus's hypothesis and confirmed his own.

The tube experiment was retried with the same result by Andreas Vesalius, whose 1543 *On the Architecture of the Human Body* was the first great advance in human anatomy after Galen and set a new standard for anatomical procedure at University of Padua. Vesalius's follower and occasional critic, Gabriel Fallopius, also agreed with Galen's finding a few years later.

William Harvey knew that he must establish the hydraulic nature of the vascular system if he were to present a convincing case for the heart circulating the blood, and this entailed defeating Galen's argument. However, when he wrote *Anatomical Exercise on the Motion of the Heart and Blood,* he judged the tube experiment too difficult to perform and left Galen's results unchallenged. He argued instead that the coincidence of the pulse with the blood spurting from a wounded artery was sufficient proof that the force of the blood had dilated the artery.

James Primrose was another physician who saw the importance of the tube experiment, and in 1630 he quoted Vesalius's account of the procedure as a refutation of Harvey's theory. In Holland, Johannes Walaeus attempted the tube experiment on a rabbit in 1641 in order to support

text continues on page 114

GALEN'S ARTERIAL TUBE EXPERIMENT

text continued from page 113

Harvey's theory, but the rabbit died before he could complete the work. Harvey persevered in his efforts to duplicate Galen's experiment, no doubt because he realized its crucial nature, and reported in 1649 that he had succeeded in implanting a tube in an artery as Galen had specified, and that he had detected a weak pulse beyond the constricted arterial covering. This

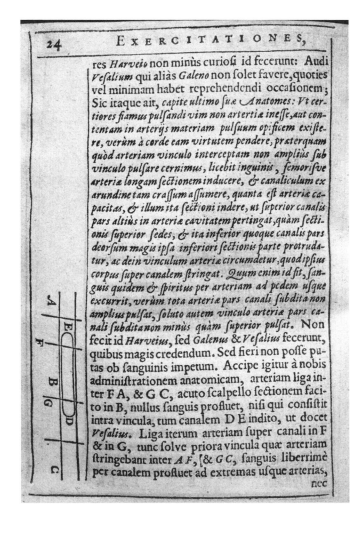

In his 1631 book Exercises and Observations on W. Harvey's Book on the Motion of the Heart and Circulation of the Blood, *James Primrose cited the arterial tube experiment performed by Galen and Vesalius as evidence that William Harvey's theory was false. In the diagram, artery AC is slit and tube ED is inserted so that the ends extend sufficiently.*

crucial experiment had finally produced the "correct" result, afterwards verified by others. What had gone wrong before?

Galen's experiment was reconstructed in 1964 under modern conditions, on the femoral artery of an anaesthetized dog. Harvey's account was confirmed, but the experimenter noted that the violent struggling of an unanaesthetized animal would have made the procedure physically difficult and resulted in a greatly elevated blood pressure, which would have aggravated bleeding and swelling, possibly obstructing the artery and obscuring observation.

A simpler crucial experiment had been devised by Fortunatus Plemp in 1654. Plemp made a small incision and carefully inserted a small sponge into the artery, blocking the blood flow. He observed that the artery no longer pulsed beyond the blockage, even though the arterial wall was continuous—a result that was consistent with Harvey's hypothesis and falsified Galen's. A good crucial experiment must be not only logically decisive, but also sufficiently manageable and repeatable to produce unambiguous results.

text continued from page 111

to move from the veins through the lungs to the arteries, but only under violent circumstances, such as extreme exercise or invasive surgery. Riolan argued that there was only a limited circulation of blood within each vascular system, and that the functions and contents of the veins and arteries remained distinct. He wholly rejected Descartes's account.

Harvey responded to Riolan in 1649 with a short treatise called *Two Anatomical Exercises on the Circulation of the Blood,* which took the form of two letters addressed to his colleague. The first of these is Harvey's response to specific criticisms that Riolan raised in his 1648 treatise. In answer to Riolan's doubts about how and why the blood passes from the arteries to the veins through the body tissues, Harvey speculated that the arterial blood pressure forces the blood into the tissues, and that the action of the body's muscles then forces the blood into the smallest veins. Against Riolan's claim that there are connecting passages, or anastomoses, that let blood flow from the veins into the arteries under certain abnormal conditions, Harvey offered an experiment, one of the few in the first letter.

An age-old method of slaughtering animals for food called for the opening of a large artery and letting the animal's blood drain as completely as possible. Harvey claimed that if the principal vein into the heart is tied off first, so that the blood cannot possibly enter the heart from the veins, then the animal's arteries will drain, but the veins will not. This would not be the case if, as Riolan and the ancient Greeks thought, the veins emptied into the arteries via anastomoses only when the arteries were unnaturally wounded. This experiment is a slight variation on one presented in the 1628 book, in which Harvey tied off the aorta next to the heart and opened a large artery, which showed that the heart was the sole source of arterial blood, but did not in itself prove that the blood came to the heart through the veins.

Riolan clearly rejected Harvey's idea of circulation, but ambiguities in Riolan's discussion of blood movement in the body allowed Harvey to interpret Riolan's views as needing only slight modifications to agree with Harvey's own findings. One can speculate that Harvey's personal friendship with Riolan and his privileged position as a French royal physician encouraged Harvey to avoid direct confrontation and criticism of his statements. Instead, he relied on a kind of rhetorical subterfuge, making his point while appearing not to contradict Riolan.

Harvey's second letter to Riolan appears to have been drafted already in the early 1640s as a response to various criticisms, and then later adapted for *Two Anatomical Exercises on the Circulation of the Blood*. The letter mentions Riolan only casually at the beginning and at the end. Unlike the first letter, which used arguments and authoritative citations to portray Riolan's views as consistent with his own, the second presented new experimental evidence and drew inferences from it, much more like his first book. He describes his successful completion of Galen's arterial tube experiment, in which a hollow, open-ended pipe was inserted into an artery to see if the pulse traveled in the artery wall rather than the blood .

Harvey's results, however, were opposite to what Galen and later anatomists had observed; the pulsing action of the artery does *not* depend on the transmission of a pulse along the arterial wall, but rather on fluctuating blood pressure. As further evidence, Harvey cited the case of a nobleman who had good pulse in his feet up until his death. However, a postmortem dissection revealed that his descending aorta, which was the source of the blood to his legs, was heavily calcified and therefore its walls had become inflexible and unable to pulsate. This evidence supported his observation that blood will pulse from a very small incision made in an artery in time with the contraction of the heart, and also confirmed his early assertion in *Anatomical Exercise on the Motion of the Heart and Blood* that the throbbing of an exposed arterial aneurism in the neck of a nobleman was caused by the force of the pulsing blood.

Harvey also answered a question raised by Johann Vesling and other correspondents and critics: If the blood in the veins and arteries is truly the same blood, constantly circulating, why is it that venous blood is a dark red, but arterial blood is bright red? Harvey again offered an experiment, one that Walaeus reported in a letter to Bartholin that was published in 1641. If similar basins are filled with arterial blood in one and blood from a vein in the other, after the blood cools for a while and begins to coagulate, the blood in both basins will have the same color. Closer examination of the clotted blood in both containers reveals no difference. Harvey proposed that arterial blood appears brighter than venous blood because it has been strained through the porous tissue of the lungs.

Harvey refused to speculate on the role of spirits in the blood, pointing out that philosophers often relied on spirits to explain what they could not see when in fact they were simply ignorant of the causes of natural phenomena. Experimental evidence was lacking—nobody had discovered spirits during dissection. Furthermore, philosophers could not even agree on whether spirits were material or immaterial essences, a choice that was complicated by theological concerns, since arguments about spirits carried implications for teachings about the holy spirit and the nature of God. Harvey had opened blood vessels underwater and saw no evidence of air bubbles or anything other than blood issuing forth; this was evidence against air entering the blood through the lungs. He acknowledged that most physicians since the ancient Greek Hippocrates believed that some sort of spirit caused activity in the body, but he did not venture further speculation on its nature.

Instead, Harvey focused on the blood itself as an agent of activity and source of vital heat. Probably in response to the claims of the Cartesians that the heart heated the blood, which in turn boiled up and caused cardiac diastole, Harvey argued that the blood heats the heart by coursing through the shortest vascular circuit of all, namely the arteries and veins in the heart itself. His own theory was that the blood had some sort of principle of fermentation, a natural capacity to effervesce like beer or wine, that caused the auricles to dilate, which in turn triggered the muscular contraction of the heart. That is, he thought it likely that diastole was caused by the innate heat of the blood, but that systole was caused by diastole, and therefore the blood's heat was the true cause of the pulse.

Despite these speculations, Harvey was committed to the experimental method in *Two Anatomical Exercises on the Circulation of the Blood*. He referred to his ideas about the heat of the blood not as a truth already factually demonstrated but as a thesis that needed to be taken up as a hypothesis for rational consideration by other researchers. He cited Aristotle to back up his contention that clear demonstrations of readily perceptible things in nature ought to be preferred over rational arguments to the contrary, and he repeated what he had written to Caspar Hofmann: He had demonstrated the circulation of the blood by experiment and by reasoned argument he had concluded that the heart was the efficient cause of circulation. There was no sense in drawing conclusions about final causes or purposes until the facts were first established; only then should one inquire about their meanings. After all, nature was older than any of the ancient medical writers, and therefore what the experimenter could learn by witnessing nature firsthand had greater authority than what Galen or even Aristotle had written.

This scientific attitude is quite like that expressed by Harvey's near contemporaries, the Italian astronomer and physicist Galileo Galilei and the Belgian medical chemist Jean Baptiste van Helmont, both of whom sought the freedom to make scientific investigations of nature and develop working theories without the censure of religious authorities who relied on what was written in old books. In both cases, their freedom to publish their scientific theories was suppressed by the Catholic church, which imposed house arrest on them, preventing them from discussing their ideas publicly. The Catholic church had no such power in England, which was Protestant.

Harvey's experimental investigation of the nature of the heart and vascular system had revealed that the blood forcefully leaves the heart and pulses out into the body's tissues, and that it returns from the body's tissues to the heart through the veins. The valves in the heart and veins are tight—he demonstrated by experiment that one cannot even blow air backwards through the valves of the veins—and therefore the blood *must* flow through the vascular system in one direction.

Harvey now brought forth additional experimental evidence to support what he had set forth earlier. When a vein in a living animal is severed, blood will freely flow from the end away from the heart, but only dribble from the end toward it; but when an artery is cut, the blood will only trickle from the end away from the heart, but violently spurt from the end toward the heart. The autopsy of an English nobleman, Sir Robert Darcy, revealed an obstruction at the outlet of the left ventricle, and Harvey concluded that the systolic force that the heart exerted on the blood, which was unable to be relieved by escape into the arteries, had caused the rupture evident in the ventricle. Such power was consistent with his theory of forceful systole. Furthermore, the blood clearly flows with considerable speed, unlike what the Cartesians and Galenists claimed.

The inescapable conclusion was that the blood *must* circulate from the arteries to the veins through the body tissues, even if the passages are too small to see, as Harvey had previously argued was the case for the lungs and for the rapid passage of fluid through the kidneys and into the bladder. Now he added another observation. He noted that the face of a criminal who had been executed by hanging was

discolored by blood that had escaped the vessels and infil-
trated the skin. When the noose was removed from the
man, the blood gradually gravitated downward to discolor
the rest of his body. Clearly blood could travel through the
tissues outside the blood vessels.

Harvey established circulation as the only logical conclusion of wide-ranging experimental evidence drawn from
both living and dead animals, including humans. The
inability to see the small linking vessels or transmission of
blood through the lung tissues did not constitute sufficient
evidence against his general argument, but counted only as
an absence of additional proof for it. Had he lived a few
years longer, he would have read Marcello Malpighi's
account of using a microscope to observe blood moving in
the capillaries of a frog's lung in 1660. In the meantime,
more and more medical scholars were becoming convinced
of circulation. By the middle of the 1650s new experiments
were being suggested to establish a role for the lungs and
blood in connection with animal heat and respiration that
supported Harvey's description of circulation.

5

Harvey's Last Years and His Legacy

Until 1649 William Harvey's professional life was dominated by the political controversy and military contests that engulfed England during the reign of King Charles I. The English Revolution and Civil War had torn the commonwealth apart, forcing many scholars to live abroad or choose sides at home. The universities were closed for long periods, and when they were open, political whims of the government disrupted teaching by changing the faculty. The king's execution failed to bring harmony to England, as members of Parliament struggled with each other and with the army for control.

In the midst of all this confusion, a new level of scientific discussion was taking place, almost as if investigation of nature's secrets by using experimental methods offered a kind of neutral ground on which scholars of various political and religious persuasions could meet. Scientists began convening informally at Gresham College in London, just as they had met and collaborated at Oxford in the 1640s. Many of them were also physicians and members of the Royal College of Physicians, which became another important meeting place for the discussion of the new science.

This deed, dated June 21, 1656, transferred ownership of the landed estate of Burmarsh in Kent, which William Harvey had inherited from his father, to the Royal College of Physicians. Income from the land provided money for an annual speech and feast at the college, as well as providing a salary for the librarian.

Despite the indignities Harvey had suffered as a Royalist—his lodgings at Whitehall were looted, and most of his medical and scientific records destroyed —politics provided no barrier to his participation in the scientific community or his continuing friendship with scholars of diverse political and religious views. Harvey's status as an internationally famous anatomist was increasingly valued by England's medical and scientific elite, many of whom he had convinced of his discovery over the years. He became a symbol for England's scientific achievement in a new age of science. Harvey never returned to St. Bartholomew's Hospital, but he became something of an elder statesman at the Royal College of Physicians, to which he turned much of his attention.

In 1651 he offered the College president a large donation to build a library and museum. The College responded favorably, and he began to carry out his plan. The expansion was completed in 1654, and to celebrate the event, Harvey signed over the deed to the new building and its contents to the College, where a bust of him was unveiled to honor his accomplishments and generosity.

He was elected the College's president, but declined the office owing to his advanced age and poor health. He was then 76 years old, and like many elderly gentlemen of his day he suffered from gout, a painful disease of the joints, and perhaps also had kidney stones. In 1656 he finally resigned the Lumley lectureship, which had been the mainstay of his academic career. He also donated his family estate in Kent to the Royal College of Physicians, with instructions that the rent be used to hire a keeper for the library and to pay for an annual oration—in Latin—and dinner for the members, in order to commemorate the College's benefactors.

William Harvey spent his last years living at the various estates of his surviving brothers, Eliab and Daniel, who owned houses in and around London. He continued to

Charles Scarburgh was William Harvey's close friend and successor as Lumley lecturer at the Royal College of Physicians. After the defeat of the Royalist forces and surrender of Oxford to the Parliamentary army, Harvey moved to London and persuaded Scarburgh to follow him, promising to help him establish a medical practice.

correspond with naturalists and physicians, but his last letters indicate that he was becoming worn out. He must have been in rather poor shape physically, for he is reported to have prepared a fatally large dose of opium and to have instructed his friend Charles Scarburgh to administer the drug to him when he requested it. However, a stroke felled him before he deemed it necessary to take his own life.

John Aubrey, whose accounts of famous Englishmen provide some anecdotal information, reported that Harvey woke up on the morning of June 3, 1657, with "palsey of the tongue" and sent for his apothecary to let blood from it. This was a typically Galenic response: relieving a surfeit of blood from the afflicted part in order to eliminate a vascular obstruction and restore function. In this case, it did little good. He died later that day, at age 79. His body was removed to Eliab's house in London, where it lay in state. Eliab had already paid to have a family chapel erected at Hempstead Church, in Essex, and on June 26 Harvey's body, wrapped in lead sheets in order to keep vermin from attacking it, was taken there and placed next to the bodies of Eliab's daughters.

In death, William Harvey was generous to his large extended family, giving various sums and pieces of his household furnishings to his nephews and nieces, their children, and their servants. He made special provisions for the continued care of his retarded nephew, Will Fowkes, the son of his sister Amy. The Harveys were a tight-knit family, and Amy's father and brothers undertook to share the costs of supporting her son. As a childless and wealthy man, William Harvey seems to have shouldered the main financial responsibility for his nephew's upkeep, as young Will is already mentioned as his "ward in lunacy" in a 1637 court record.

Harvey bequeathed his precious silver surgical instruments and his favorite velvet gown to his friend and successor in the Lumley lectureship, Charles Scarburgh. His books, papers, and best Persian rug he left to the College of Physicians. What remained of his properties, along with one of his most prized possessions, his coffee pot, he bequeathed to his brother Eliab. Coffee was new to England in the 17th century, and Harvey was in the vanguard in drinking it. Before London's first coffeehouse opened, he and Eliab had enjoyed pleasant conversation over many a cup of coffee from that pot.

After Harvey's death, the College of Physicians continued to take an active role as a focal point of the new scientific research that took shape in England in the second half of the century. Harvey had helped train the new generation of anatomists, who were part of a Europe-wide effort to examine closely the various organs and attempt to redefine how the human body works and how diseases affect its operation. Harvey's successors—Ralph Bathurst, Thomas Willis, Robert Boyle, Robert Hooke, and Richard Lower—abandoned the last vestiges of Galenic cardio-pulmonary physiology and accepted Harvey's assertion on the function for the heart—the mechanical circulation of the blood through the lungs and the rest of the body.

In London, the excitement of the new scientific age was dimmed briefly by a serious outbreak in 1665 of bubonic plague, which took a great toll on the city's population. In 1666 the Great Fire of London burned the city, and the Royal College of Physicians and Harvey's library and museum were destroyed. But Harvey's most valuable legacy, his ideas and his example, were unscathed—the international scientific community used them as the basis for a new model of how animal organisms function.

William Harvey has been celebrated on various postage stamps from around the world. This 1978 stamp from the Soviet Union commemorates 400 years since his birth.

HARVEY'S DISCOVERY AND THE ABANDONMENT OF ANCIENT MEDICAL THEORY

William Harvey understood very well that his discovery of blood circulation in the body meant the existing theories of how the body and its parts functioned had to be revised. He had fatally wounded the ancient physiological doctrine of Galen, which had been taught in Europe's universities since their inception, but he had not offered a replacement for it.

True, he had suggested some directions for future research at the end of *Anatomical Exercise on the Motion of the Heart and Blood in Animals* by pointing out that circulation required a new view of how poisons, medications, and diseases affect the body. But in many respects Harvey was still a Renaissance natural philosopher, wedded to ideas and perspectives that were not conducive to the revisions that his work had made necessary.

Medical students of the next generation, however, were not limited to the teachings of Aristotle and Galen, but were exposed to new natural philosophies that were elaborated and debated during the middle decades of the 17th century. The chemical theories of the Paracelsian physicians, followers of the German physician Paracelsus who rejected Galen's humors and spoke of the body as a kind of chemical laboratory, were gaining acceptance in learned circles in England. More importantly, perhaps, Descartes's "mechanical" idea that everything in the tangible world was governed by mathematical and physical laws was also becoming prominent.

In practice, students combined ideas from various philosophers, creating a "mechanical" version of Paracelsian chemical theory. According to this new theory, all changes were fundamentally chemical changes, but rather than being attributable to spirits, they occurred because of mechanical collisions, combinations, dissolutions, and recombinations of microscopic bodies called corpuscles. This idea was especially important in England in the second half of the 17th century, and it shaped how Harvey's followers imagined the human body to work.

According to corpuscular philosophy, all materials—blood, for example—were composed of corpuscles (little bodies) or molecules (little masses). These particles joined together to form invisible structures that explained the properties and functions of visible things. Armed with theories such as this that probed beyond the four causes of Aristotelian entities and supported research into the fine structures of the organs, fluids, and solid parts of plants and animals, scientists of the generations after Harvey were able to construct a replacement for Galenic physiology and redirect medical research to investigation of the body's microstructure and microfunction that continues today.

The problem raised by Harvey's discovery that attracted the most attention during the second half of the 17th century was the nature and purpose of respiration. Harvey's work spurred investigations into the nature of the blood, the composition of the air, and the role of the lungs. These lines of research eventually brought physiology into closer contact with physics and chemistry, laying the foundations for modern medical science.

Oxford University, where Harvey had spent several years prior to the town's surrender to Parliamentary forces in June 1646, was the seat of the most diligent pursuit of the new physiology. Harvey had worked with and influenced a number of young medical scholars at Oxford, many of whom continued his initiative after his death.

The Next Generation

After the Royalists surrendered at the end of the Civil War, education at Oxford University resumed, and a new generation of medical scholars focused on new problems in anatomy that arose from Harvey's discovery of circulation. Researchers were interested in following up on the new questions raised by Harvey's work and thought up new experiments to ascertain the function of the heart, blood, and lungs in respiration and nutrition and explained these functions in terms of the movements and reactions of chemical substances. Experiments of injections, and even transfusions, were conducted during the next couple of decades to determine how respiration and circulation worked and how the blood affected the health of the body. These experiments were conducted at Oxford University and the Royal Society in London, which was founded in 1660 specifically to further experimental science. The English were not alone in this research—a German medical author even advocated human injections as a possible form of therapy. However, in England the procedures were linked explicitly with investigations that followed up on problems that directly resulted from Harvey's discovery.

The first attempt to inject blood from one animal to another was made by Francis Potter. He used a bladder that was fitted with various ivory tubes and hollow quills as a kind of primitive injection syringe. In 1656 Robert Boyle, Christopher Wren, and other medical researchers injected opium into a vessel in a dog's leg, which stupefied it for a time. Wren, who later became famous as a mathematician and architect of St. Paul's Cathedral in London, was an avid physiologist. He extended these injection experiments to include wine and ale, which caused the dog to become intoxicated and to urinate—exactly what one would expect from the effects of alcohol in a human.

In 1657 Wren and his colleague Timothy Clarke experimented by injecting a toxic metallic compound that was used by physicians to cause vomiting into one of the French Ambassador's servants (who presumably had little choice in the matter). When the servant fainted right away, they immediately quit the experiment and went back to using animals. By the early 1660s Thomas Willis and another Oxford physiologist Richard Lower started injecting ink, milk, and other colored substances into freshly-killed animals to trace the blood flow in the brain and liver. Lower also injected milk into an artery to see if the blood returning in the associated vein appeared milky, which it did. Although circulation was not in doubt by that time, it was excellent experimental proof that the blood flowed from the ends of the arteries into the veins.

These young experimental physiologists realized that the new techniques for injection and transfusion could lead to feeding and resuscitating animals and even people artificially. This offered new possibilities for medical therapy, even for prolongation of life. In 1664 Lower tried to feed a dog intravenously with warm milk, but it died within the hour. He speculated that sheep blood might be useful to replace blood lost by humans who suffered traumatic injuries or surgery, if the procedural details of transfusion could be worked out. In

1666 Lower finally succeeded by piping blood from an artery to a vein, taking advantage of the higher arterial blood pressure to push the blood through the tube. The recipient of this new method of transfusion survived.

A problem connected in determining the role of the blood was the function of the lungs. Harvey had argued that the vitality of the blood did not require anything from the air during respiration, and believed that the lungs chiefly served to cool the blood and mechanically strain it, making it more homogeneous. Many of his followers, however, supposed that respiration served to provide some sort of material substance, upon which life depended, and perhaps also functioned to rid the blood of undesirable waste fumes. In 1667 Robert Boyle, a prominent experimentalist in the second-half of 17th century, planned a crucial experiment to settle the debate about whether the lungs were effective mainly because they moved mechanically or because they permitted air to enter the blood and mix with it chemically. This experiment, and those that followed closely to help clarify how the lungs worked and what role the air played, exemplify the rapid pace of experimental design and execution that characterized English science in the second half of 17th century and eventually resulted in the solidification of Harvey's findings.

Robert Hooke, a scientist and assistant to Robert Boyle, and Richard Lower conducted Boyle's experiment before the Royal Society later that year. First they opened a live dog and connected a bellows to its trachea, so that they could inflate the lungs mechanically in an in-and-out pumping action. They demonstrated that when they ceased to inflate the lungs mechanically, the dog began to go into convulsions, but when they resumed inflating the lungs, the dog returned to its normal state. Then they added a novelty: they fitted the dog with a double bellows, so that when one was opening the other was closing, which provided a continuous stream of air into the lungs. To provide an exit for the air, they punctured the lower ends of the lungs. In this way, air was constantly forced into the lungs, which no longer expanded and contracted, yet the heart continued to beat as usual. This demonstrated that it was the supply of air and not the motion of the lungs that was necessary to respiration. Based on this experiment, in 1668 Hooke designed an experiment that forced a dog to inhale and exhale the same air over and over into a bladder. When the dog began to die, the bladder was removed and the dog revived. Hooke proved that fresh air was necessary to respiration.

Richard Lower, perhaps the most brilliant of the Oxford anatomists, effectively completed the work on the action and uses of the heart and blood that Harvey had begun. Starting in autumn 1667 he conducted a series of physiological experiments to verify the findings of earlier physiological experiments and organized them in a coherent explanation. He published it in *A Treatise on the Heart* in 1669. This was a book that Harvey would have approved, not only because it was based on his work, but also because its method of proof consisted of an accumulation of experimental and observational evidence and was largely devoid of speculation about causes. Lower also improved on Harvey's famous quantitative calculation, bringing more precision to the argument. Richard Lower's work in *A Treatise on the Heart* did not put an end to the creation of new theories that addressed the many discoveries revealed by observation and experimentation in the wake of Harvey's revolution. In time, new ideas about the composition of atmospheric air and the role of heat in animal metabolism would lead to an even better understanding of respiration. Nevertheless, it is evident that all of this research unfolded as a direct consequence of Harvey's striking discovery and the careful experimental methods by which he demonstrated circulation. It is for this reason that he is regarded as one of the key founders of modern science.

CHRONOLOGY

April 1, 1578
William Harvey is born at Folkestone in Kent, England

Summer 1597
Harvey is awarded a bachelor's degree by the University of Cambridge

Fall 1599
Harvey travels to Italy to study at the University of Padua

April 25, 1602
Harvey is granted the M.D. for his study at the University of Padua

1604
Harvey marries Elizabeth Browne

1607
Harvey is admitted as a Fellow to the Royal College of Physicians in London

1609
Harvey is appointed physician at St. Bartholomew's Hospital in London

August 1615
Harvey is appointed Lumley Lecturer at the Royal College of Physicians; he gives his first lecture on April 16, 1616

February 3, 1618
Harvey is appointed Extraordinary Physician to King James I

1628
Harvey's *Anatomical Exercise on the Motion of the Heart and Blood in Animals* is published

1639

Harvey is appointed Senior Physician to King Charles I

1649

Harvey's *Two Anatomical Exercises on the Circulation of the Blood* is published; King Charles I is executed

1651

Harvey's *On the Generation of Animals* is published

1654

Harvey is elected to the presidency of the Royal College of Physicians, but turns it down

1656

Harvey resigns the Lumley Lectureship, donates his patrimonial estate to the Royal College of Physicians, and retires

June 3, 1657

William Harvey dies of a stroke at age 79

1660

Experimental philosophers gather to form the Royal Society

1669

Richard Lower's *Treatise on the Heart* finishes the work that Harvey had begun with the publication of *Anatomical Exercise On the Motion of the Heart and Blood*

Harvey's Works in Translation

Harvey, William. *The Anatomical Exercises. De Motu Cordis and De Circulatione Sanguinis in English Translation.* New York: Dover, 1995.

———. *The Works of William Harvey.* Trans. Robert Willis. Arthur C. Guyton. Philadelphia: University of Pennsylvania Press, 1989.

———. *Lectures on the Whole of Anatomy: An Annotated Translation of Prelectiones Anatomiae Universalis.* Ed. and trans. C. D. O'Malley, F. N. L. Poynter, and K. F. Russell. Berkeley: University of California Press, 1961.

———. *The Circulation of the Blood and Other Writings.* Trans. Kenneth J. Franklin. London: Dent and Sons, 1963.

———. *An Anatomical Disputation Concerning the Movement of the Heart and Blood in Living Creatures.* Ed. and trans. Gweneth Whitteridge. Oxford: Blackwell, 1976.

———. *De Motu Locali Animalium 1627.* Ed. and trans. Gweneth Whitteridge. Cambridge: Cambridge University Press, 1959.

———. *Disputations Touching the Generation of Animals.* Ed. and trans. Gweneth Whitteridge. Oxford: Blackwell, 1981.

———. *William Harvey, The Anatomical Lectures.* Ed. and trans. Gweneth Whitteridge. London: Livingstone, 1964.

Books on Harvey, His Work, and His Times

Bylebyl, Jerome J., ed. *William Harvey and His Age: The Professional and Social Context of the Discovery of the Circulation.* Baltimore: John Hopkins University Press, 1979.

Chaubois, Louis. *William Harvey: His Life and Times, His Discoveries, His Methods.* New York: Philosophical Library, 1957. Translated from an early French biography.

Frank, Robert G. *Harvey and the Oxford Physiologists: Scientific Ideas and Social Interaction.* Berkeley: University of California Press, 1980.

French, Roger Kenneth. *William Harvey's Natural Philosophy.* Cambridge: Cambridge University Press, 1994.

Hamburger, Jean. *The Diary of William Harvey.* Trans. Barbara Wright. New Brunswick, N.J.: Rutgers University Press, 1992.

Keele, Kenneth David. *William Harvey; the Man, the Physician, and the Scientist.* London: Thomas Nelson and Sons, 1965.

Keynes, Geoffrey. *The Life of William Harvey.* Oxford: Clarendon Press, 1966.

————. *The Portraiture of William Harvey.* London: Royal College of Surgeons of London, 1949.

Power, D'Arcy. *William Harvey.* 1898. Reprint, New York: Heirs of Hippocrates Library, 1995.

Royal Society of Medicine, Historical Section. *Portraits of Dr. William Harvey.* Oxford: Oxford University Press, 1913.

Simpson, R. R. *Shakespeare and Medicine.* Edinburgh and London: E. & S. Livingstone, 1962.

Whitteridge, Gweneth. *William Harvey and the Circulation of the Blood.* London: Macdonald, 1971.

Yount, Lisa. *William Harvey: Discoverer of How Blood Circulates.* Hillside, N.J.: Enslow, 1994.

INDEX

ACKNOWLEDGMENTS

I wish to thank Professor Dr. Guenter B. Risse, M.D. Ph.D. for introducing me to the history of medicine while I was an undergraduate student at the University of Wisconsin. His breadth of interest, depth of scholarship, and personal concern for the teaching of medical history have been an inspiration.

PICTURE CREDITS

British Library, Italian Manuscripts: 27; Guildhall Library, London: 19, 34; Heritage Room Folkestone Library & Museum: 13; Huntington Library: 97; Laserwords: 46, 51, 57, 60; Library of Congress: 16 (LF128.L7), 36 (LC-USZ62-83233), 75 (LC-D416-128), 79 (LF528.L7), 80 (LC-USZ62-77770); Metropolitan Museum of Art (Bredius 478): 23; Moody Medical: 127; National Library of Medicine: Cover (Background) (B029256), Cover (Inset) (B029255), Frontispiece (B029254), 25 (A1629), 29 (A012640), 31 (A026925), 44 (A012195), 63 (A012719), 70 (MS A 44.I, fol. 1b), 83 (A012109), 103 (A016203), 104 (B014976), 108 (B05094), 111 (B011782); New York Academy of Medicine: 42, 53, 55, 56, 114; Royal College of Medicine: 34, 40, 76, 85, 93 Permission from British Library, 123, 125; St. Bartholomew's Hospital: 72; Wellcome Library: 88; Yale Medical Historical Library: 66; Zentralbibliothek Zurich: 21

AUTHORS

Jole Shackelford is assistant professor in the Program for the History of Medicine and Biological Sciences at the University of Minnesota.

Owen Gingerich is Professor of Astronomy and of the History of Science at the Harvard–Smithsonian Center for Astrophysics in Cambridge, Massachusetts. The author of more than 400 articles and reviews, he has also written *The Great Copernicus Chase and Other Adventures in Astronomical History* and *The Eye of Heaven: Ptolomy, Copernicus, Kepler.*